A GUIDE TO COPYRIGHT FOR MUSEUMS AND GALLERIES

This is the indispensable reference tool for everyone in museums and galleries who has to deal with questions of copyright. It shows that, when properly handled, copyright is more than an administrative burden – it can provide opportunities for institutions to achieve their core objectives. The user-friendly guide comprehensively addresses issues such as:

- What is copyright?

- How long does copyright last?

- How can you make money from copyright and other intellectual property rights?

- What are the consequences of unauthorised use?

A wealth of practical advice and information is offered, including a series of photocopiable sample legal agreements which cover matters such as filming, publishing, licensing rights and multimedia issues.

Written by a team of legal experts on copyright, *A Guide to Copyright for Museums and Galleries* will be an invaluable resource for busy professionals. It is published in association with the UK Museums Copyright Group, and supported and endorsed by the Museums and Galleries Commission and the Scottish Museums Council.

Silver Favourites by Sir Lawrence Alma-Tadema (1836–1912) © Manchester City Art Galleries

A straightforward example of an art photograph of a two-dimensional artistic work. The copyright in the painting has expired since the artist died over 70 years ago, so there are no special considerations attached to obtaining a licence from the artist's estate to reproduce the picture. The copyright in the photograph will expire 70 years after the death of the photographer.

A Guide to Copyright for Museums and Galleries

Peter Wienand, Anna Booy and Robin Fry

London and New York

First published 2000
by Routledge
11 New Fetter Lane, London EC4P 4EE

Simultaneously published in the USA and Canada
by Routledge
29 West 35th Street, New York, NY 10001

Routledge is an imprint of the Taylor & Francis Group

Typeset in Sabon by Florence Production Ltd, Stoodleigh, Devon.
Printed and bound in Great Britain by TJ International Ltd, Padstow, Cornwall

British Library Cataloguing in Publication Data
A catalogue record for this book is available from the British Library

Library of Congress Cataloging in Publication Data
Wienand, Peter, 1963–
A guide to copyright for museums and galleries / Peter Wienand, Anna Booy,
and Robin Fry.
p. cm.
Includes bibliographical references and index.
1. Copyright–Art–Great Britain. 2. Museums–Law and legislation–
Great Britain. I. Booy, Anna. II. Fry, Robin, 1955– III. Title.
KD1320 .W53 2000
346.4104'82–dc21
99–053485

ISBN 0–415–21721–0

Contents

Acknowledgements

We have received innumerable expressions of support and encouragement while writing this guide. First and foremost we must thank the members of the executive committee of the Museums Copyright Group, without whose help and enthusiasm this guide might never have seen the light of day: Patrick Wright, Michael Cass, Margaret Greeves, Celia Clear, Jane Carmichael, Emma Williams, Sophie Sutherland, Geoffrey Matthews, Angela Murphy and Jane Ryder. We owe a particular debt of gratitude to Heather Wilson of the Museums and Galleries Commission, who was among the first to see the need for the Museums Copyright Group and the guide – the assistance of that Commission has been instrumental. Liz McRobb and Andrew Keir of Shepherd and Wedderburn WS have provided an invaluable appendix on the law in Scotland. We must thank Vicky Peters, our commissioning editor, for her vision in taking on this guide and her encouragement to us throughout. We are also especially grateful to all those who took the time to read parts of the text and comment on it, in particular Leslie Cram of the Museum of Reading. We each have to thank our firms for giving us the time to write this guide, and our colleagues for all their help and patience. Finally we have all relied hugely on the tolerance of our families, who have given us the space and time to do what we could not do in working hours (what were those?): we have each to find our way of thanking them.

Peter Wienand, Anna Booy, Robin Fry
February 2000

Statement of the law

This guide is written in accordance with the law in force in the United Kingdom as at 1 July 1999.

Appendix 4.4 contains a survey of the law in Scotland as it applies to copyright and related areas.

Certain changes in the law of copyright in the United Kingdom may be envisaged upon implementation of the proposed EC Directive on Copyright and Related Rights in the Information Society (see Appendix 4.5).

Museums in receipt of public funding and all museums registered with the Museums and Galleries Commission should aim to offer the widest possible physical, sensory and intellectual access to their collections ... subject to the resources available to them.

(DCMS Consultation paper published December 1997)

1. Introduction

Interior, The Tate Gallery St Ives © Tate Gallery, London

The representations of the sculptures are unlikely to be held to be 'incidental inclusions' in the photograph and so permission to reproduce the sculptures would ordinarily need to be obtained from the sculptors or their estates (a representation in two dimensions of a three-dimensional work requiring a licence). The same may be true of the building, as a work of architecture. However, making a photograph of (i) buildings and (ii) any sculptures that are permanently situated in a public place or in premises open to the public does not infringe copyright. Nor does issuing copies of such a photograph to the public.

1.1 WHY IS COPYRIGHT IMPORTANT TO MUSEUMS AND GALLERIES?

Museums are in the business of purveying information. Of course, in the days when many of our great institutions were founded, this was seen primarily in terms of providing physical access to objects which ordinary people might otherwise never see – either because they did not have the privilege of going on the Grand Tour, or because they did not have access to the great private collections built up (in many cases) by those who had.

Today, the role of museums and galleries is seen as wider than simply allowing people to see objects. We still regard the direct physical experience of the great artefacts of human cultural and scientific endeavour as having some special quality. But museums and galleries see their mission as more than warehousing a collection of old objects. They are educational institutions in the widest sense. The new technologies, especially digital networking technologies, allow a more ambitious view of this mission. But the wider conception goes back a long way, before the Internet had been dreamt of. It is currently reflected in the statutory objectives of some of our great national institutions. The Acts of Parliament which established the Boards of Trustees of such institutions as the Science Museum, the Tate Gallery and the National Gallery specifically enjoined the Trustees 'generally (to) promote the public's enjoyment and under-standing', not simply of the objects in their collections, but of the fields of artistic or scientific endeavour which their collections illuminate (the National Heritage Act 1983 and the Museums and Galleries Act 1992).

Museums and galleries, then, are under a duty to communicate to the public something about their collections and the cultures that made them and the objects in them. They are, in short, in the business of publishing. Clearly there is a commercial dimension to this which we examine below, but the business of communicating to the public is at the heart of museums' and galleries' primary mission. This mission is clearly central to the existence of museums and galleries, both in defining their role, and also in justifying the special status which most museums and galleries enjoy, in the United Kingdom, as charities.

Communication to the public presupposes a number of activities:

1 the museum's or gallery's objects themselves need to be reproduced in some form so that images of them can be disseminated;

2 explanatory text needs to be created to assist in a greater enjoyment and understanding of the objects;

3 images of other objects may need to be reproduced to help put the first images in context.

All of these activities involve copyright. Reproduction is at the heart of copy-right – which is a law designed to prevent unauthorised reproduction. At the same time, the creation of original works brings into being material that is protected by copyright. So museums and galleries cannot fulfil one of their primary functions without being fundamentally affected by the law of copy-right.

Copyright evolved in England at about the time when the first of our great museums and galleries were being founded. The basic principles of our copyright law were established during the eighteenth century, first in relation to published texts, later in relation to artistic works (Hogarth was a prime mover in getting the courts to recognise the need for protection of artistic works from unauthorised copying).

Copyright is, in essence, a legal monopoly protecting certain kinds of works against unauthorised copying which, at its worst, amounts to piracy. Among the kinds of works protected by copyright are artistic works, such as paintings, drawings, engravings and the like, as well as photographs, and textual works such as books, essays, articles and so on.

So, returning briefly to the activities of museums and galleries which we identified before:

1 if the objects which need to be reproduced are still in copyright (for example, any modern paintings, or many hitherto unpublished works), then permission to copy needs to be obtained from the copyright owner;

2 the explanatory text will enjoy copyright protection, and the right to reproduce the text will need to be obtained;

3 reproduction of the images of other objects will need the licence of the copyright owners.

These examples only scratch the surface, but they should be enough to show how important it is for museums and galleries to be aware of copyright and how it affects their activities.

1.2 THE COMMERCIAL ISSUES

It may be assumed at the outset from these few examples that copyright is simply an administrative burden to museums and galleries. And, often enough, it is. The publication of a museum catalogue can involve an unexpectedly large amount of work on copyright matters such as obtaining licences or assignments of copyright.

Copyright law currently provides no exceptions (as it does for libraries) allowing museums and galleries to pursue their primary objectives without – where necessary – securing the requisite copyright permissions.

So on one level, copyright can involve a cost to museums and galleries, often in the form of copyright fees and royalties.

However, museums and galleries may be able to reduce that cost by judicious management of copyright. They may even be able to turn their efforts into a source of revenue, and thus find that copyright is a means of contributing funds to hard-pressed museum budgets. Copyright is (at least in some senses) an economic right, because it protects the income stream of the copyright owner from the effects of unauthorised copying of his work. Museums and galleries can sit on both sides of the fence: they may need to negotiate with copyright owners such as artists or artists' estates. But, by dint of careful management, they may also be able to acquire copyrights themselves, for example in the photographs or digitisations of the objects in their collections. These copyrights can be a valuable source of income.

1.3 STEWARDSHIP OF OUR NATIONAL HERITAGE

This may well smack of an unwelcome intrusion of commercial values in the context of museums' and galleries' public educational role.

But museums and galleries are repositories of unrivalled content for the new media. They are only one group among many who wish to publish that content, and for most of the others, the considerations applying to such publishing are purely commercial. They see the contents of museums and galleries as material for exploitation. Museums and galleries may share some of the proceeds of that exploitation, but equally they may not.

This is not to say that commercial publishing ventures are always to be spurned. For many institutions, collaborative ventures with commercial partners may be the only way of funding publishing programmes. But museums and galleries should still take care that they negotiate the best terms in such arrangements. If not, they may find either that they have lost the leverage which possession of their collections may have given them in securing copyrights in reproductions of the objects, and that commercial publishers have obtained images which they can reproduce without any return to the museum or gallery or, in the worst case, that they may not even be able to reproduce the objects in their own collections without obtaining the permission of the commercial publishers.

Some might argue that this does not matter. After all, if images are being disseminated, albeit by commercial publishers, are not the objectives of museums and galleries being fulfilled?

There are several possible answers to this:

1 Museums and galleries may consider that they have resources, for example in the form of their curators, which enables them to fulfil their duty to advance the enjoyment and understanding of the public in a way that perhaps not all commercial publishers can. It follows that greater control of the copyrights involved in disseminating images and information about their collections would assist museums and galleries in fulfilling that duty.

2 Greater control of the copyrights involved would also allow museums and galleries to exert greater control in such matters as quality of reproduction and indeed in establishing a hierarchy of different qualities for different purposes.

3 The trustees of museums and galleries have overriding duties, arising out of the status of museums and galleries as charitable trusts, to safeguard and conserve the assets of the charity, and to exploit them in a manner consistent with the objectives of the charity. This means that, if the museum or gallery owns any copyrights, then it must exploit them for the purposes of the museum or gallery. Indeed, it is arguable that in some cases the duties of the trustees extend further to preventing rights such as publication

4

right (see section 3.4 below) from falling into the hands of third parties in such a way that those third parties might be able to stop the museum or gallery from fulfilling its objectives.

4   Finally, if they can secure greater control over copyright, museums and galleries can establish for themselves whether and how far they wish to pursue non-commercial or educational policies whereby certain uses of their copyright materials are permitted at low rates or even for no payment.

1.4   COMMERCIAL EXPLOITATION *CAN* BE THE HANDMAID OF STEWARDSHIP

In this context, conserving and if possible improving the museum's copyright position runs parallel to the tasks of conservation and display that lie at the traditional heart of the museum's role.

But it is also the case that, to the extent that museums or galleries are able to acquire greater control over copyright (including copyright in their objects and images of their objects), so they should be in a better position to exploit those copyrights commercially. Merchandising and the like become possibilities. Provided that the museum or gallery's trading arm or trading subsidiary controls such exploitation, some or all of the money that is earned from such activities is always channelled back to the museum or gallery. In this way it helps to fund the primary tasks of the museum. In a world where government grants are shrinking and there is greater than ever competition for sponsorship revenues and lottery money, the exploitation of museums' and galleries' content can be a source of funding which helps to pay curators' salaries and the costs of conserving objects.

This guide is intended to help museums and galleries to learn about the impact which copyright can have on their activities. It should help to warn against the dangers that can befall the unwary traveller. But we hope that it will also help to show that copyright is more than simply an administrative burden or, at worst, an irrelevance. Properly handled, copyright can provide opportunities for museums and galleries and help them to achieve their core objectives.

1.5   HOW TO USE THIS GUIDE

This guide is divided into the following sections:

* Chapter 2 (What is copyright?) sets out the ground rules of the copyright system. It approaches the subject from first principles, and can be dipped into, or read in one go for an overview. You may find it helpful to refer back to this chapter after reading chapter 3.

* Chapter 3 (Current issues and practical solutions) is designed to apply the basic principles set out in chapter 2 to specific problems of concern to museums and galleries. It addresses particular issues from a practical perspective.

* Chapter 4 (Appendices) contains suggestions for further reading, and details of organisations that you may wish to contact for more information about

copyright. It also contains a series of sample agreements tailored for use by museums. Finally, it contains an important section on possible prospective changes to copyright law.

2. What is copyright?

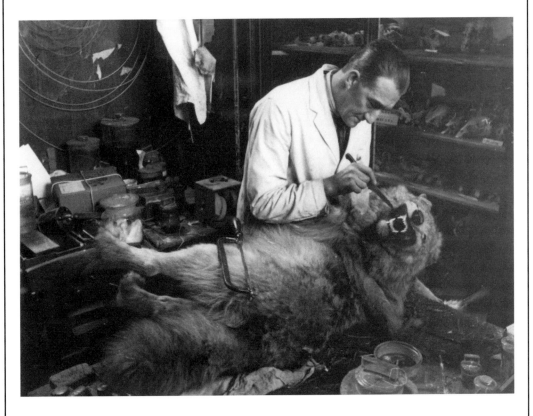

Taxidermist at Work at the Natural History Museum, London, c. 1930 © The Natural History Museum, London

Whether the photograph remains in copyright would have to be determined by reference to the principles governing the duration of copyright (section 2.3), and in particular the extension and revival of copyright in older works. The age of the photograph must mean that it remains in copyright, at least in the EU, at least until 2000 and probably for longer. There is no case law to suggest that the product of the taxidermist's skill is a 'work of artistic craftsmanship' protected by copyright.

2.1 THE FUNDAMENTALS

The family of rights

Copyright is a member of the family of legal rights, which in recent times have come to be known generally as 'intellectual property' rights. This family of rights includes some well-known rights such as patents and trade marks, as well as some peculiar rights which will be less familiar to most, such as plant breeder's rights and the rights protecting semiconductor chips.

It is perfectly possible, indeed it is quite common, for several different sorts of intellectual property rights to co-exist in the same work or product, or for several forms of the same type of rights to co-exist. A new type of branded folding chair may well contain patent rights, copyright and trade mark rights, while products such as films and multimedia CD-ROMs very often contain many separate copyrights, all owned by different entities. (This is not the same as 'joint' copyright – see section 2.4.)

Territorial restrictions and differences

One of the most important general features of intellectual property rights, including copyright, is the fact that they are 'creatures' of each different nation's laws. Rights attaching to owners of copyright therefore differ, depending on the laws of the territory being used to interpret or enforce the copyright. While there are superficial levels of similarity between the laws of some countries, the detail of these laws differs considerably.

For example, the laws of what are loosely termed 'common law' countries (such as the UK, USA, Canada and Australia) tend to treat copyright as primarily an economic right. Consequently, such countries are inclined to grant copyright protection to quite utilitarian forms of work such as train time-tables. These countries also rarely place legislative obstacles in the way of transfers or assignments of copyright. Indeed, most have specific provisions or doctrines which facilitate the transfer of copyright from employees to their employers. In the case of the USA, a doctrine called 'work for hire' applies. This assists the transfer of rights from some commissioned authors to the commissioner.

By contrast, the laws of continental European countries, such as France and Germany, tend to regard copyright more as a right protecting the personality of the author. As a result, copyright protection is unlikely to be granted to works such as train timetables, where 'personality' does not make its mark and has no function. These laws also tend to resist the easy transfer of author's rights because the author is clearly the most appropriate person to take advantage of their right of personality. (See section 2.2 on originality.)

This 'personality' approach created considerable difficulties with the protection to be given to computer software in the 1980s. It is hard to see 'personality' in lines of computer code. Even a common law country (Australia) initially refused to grant copyright protection to something as functional as software and the German courts also predictably refused it. Nevertheless, international pressure and a European Directive (91/250) subsequently required that EU member states protect computer programs by copyright as 'literary works', where the program is the author's own intellectual creation. No other criteria, such as 'personality' or 'creativity' are to be applied to determine the eligibility for software protection.

The same cannot be said for artistic works or photographs of such works however; and there are still likely to be differences in the levels of originality or creativity necessary for copyright to exist in works across Europe.

Many of the difficulties associated with different countries' laws granting different protection to different created works have been remedied by several international conventions. The most well-known international copyright conventions are the Berne Convention and the Universal Copyright Convention. Without these conventions, artistic works made by foreigners and published abroad would not be protected in the United Kingdom. Thanks to these conventions however, it is now rare for foreign works to have no protection in this country. It is also rare for UK works to be unprotected if published and exploited abroad, although it is still possible to find countries where protection given to UK nationals is low or non-existent. Some countries, for example, require copyright to be registered with national intellectual property offices, before it can be enforced, and in those countries which adhere to the Universal Copyright Convention, use of the © symbol accompanied by the name of the copyright owner and year of first publication is strongly advisable.

These differences in the extent of copyright protection internationally and the ability to enforce such protection, have always been a difficulty facing international publishers of material. The difficulties have been exacerbated by the truly global utilisation of copyright works via media such as satellite or the Internet (see section 3.6).

Not a 'positive' right

Most forms of intellectual property rights act by virtue of allowing their owners to prevent others from doing certain things. That is, the owner of the right has the 'exclusive right' to do specific acts with the subject matter of the right and therefore is in a position to ask a court to restrain others. In the UK, in the case of copyright (with which this book is primarily concerned), the exclusive rights granted include the right to copy, to issue copies to the public (often called the right to 'publish'), the right to rent or lend the work, the right to perform, show or play the work in public, to broadcast the work (or include in a cable programme) or to adapt the work. These rights are considered in more detail in section 2.5.

It must be remembered that the mere right to stop others from engaging in these activities is not necessarily the same as a positive right in the owners of the right to do the act in respect of a particular work themselves. As we have seen, there may be several rights-holders associated with a work. While each of them has the right to stop the others and third parties from engaging in the 'exclusive' rights, each will also need the consent of the others before engaging in the act of exploitation themselves.

Not ownership of the work itself

A second important fundamental limit on all intellectual property rights is the fact that they exist totally separately from the rights to the physical property in the work itself. This means that legal ownership of a work of art does not in itself enable the owner to reproduce the work of art. That is a right controlled by the owner of the copyright in the work. It is very common for the copyright in a work to be owned by someone quite different from the legal owner of the work. Libraries, for example, own many books, but very few would own the copyright in such books, and they therefore require a form of permission in order to copy portions of any book. Similarly, while museums and galleries own the physical property in many valuable works of art, the ownership of copyright in the work will not usually also pass to the museum or gallery without special legal provision being made for this – see section 2.4. It also follows, of course, that ownership of copyright does not carry with it ownership of the physical work itself.

One useful exception to this general rule concerns unpublished works which are left under a will, where the will makes no reference to copyright in the work. In such a case, the will is to be construed as including the copyright in the work, so far as the testator was the owner of the copyright immediately prior to death. This applies where the owner dies after 1 August 1989, but irrespective of when the work was created. Slightly different provisions apply where the owner died before August 1989, and specific legal advice should be taken on such a case. (Differences may also exist in the case of bequests of engravings, woodcuts, sculptures and works of artistic craftsmanship.) This means that if a bequest was made to Museum A of 'all my paintings' while a residual bequest of 'all my personal property' went to Gallery B, then copyright in the paintings would, provided the will said nothing else about the disposition of copyright, go to Museum A.

Not an absolute monopoly right

Another important limitation on the rights associated with copyright (but not all intellectual property rights) is that while 'copying' is protected, the law of copyright does not act against those who independently develop, without copying, the same or a similar work. In this respect, copyright is known as only a 'relative' monopoly rather than an 'absolute' monopoly. This means, for example, that a photographer taking a photograph of a scene from a particularly clever vantage point, cannot use copyright in the resulting photography to prevent others from unknowingly or innocently creating an identical or similar photograph from the same vantage point. If a second photographer used the first photograph as a guide to preparing the copy then the legal position would be quite different.

A special exception to the rule against copying is provided under UK law specifically for artists; where an artist of a work has transferred the copyright to a third party, the artist does not infringe that copyright by copying the work in making another artistic work, provided the main design of the earlier work is not repeated or imitated.

10

Not a protection of fundamental ideas in the work

It is commonly said about copyright that it does not exist to protect 'ideas as such', but only the 'particular expression of ideas'. This is a difficult doctrine, particularly in the UK where it has not been clearly developed. Many grey areas exist. Perhaps the best way of looking at the distinction between the 'an idea as such' and the 'expression of an idea' is to see them as existing at either end of a scale. At some point on the scale between the two, copying will become an infringement of copyright in the work.

A good example is looking at the copyright in a book. While it is clear that total reproduction of the book by another is an infringement, it is less clear that an infringement exists if only various aspects of the overall plot are taken. Many fictional books can be characterised as having the same broad plot; for example 'boy meets girl, they fall in love, they have a disagreement, they are reconciled and boy marries girl'. No one would suggest that any copyright exists in such a plot. (Under US law, this is certainly because of the 'idea/expression' dichotomy. Under UK law it may just be that it would be difficult to prove that an author had not independently invented their own plot, it being not a plot that requires much imagination.) Some plots however are more specific and unusual and independent invention therefore seems less likely. Copyright is likely to exist in them.

This doctrine, and the rule in favour of independent creation can combine to make it possible to an extent to subvert copyright if one is determined to do so. For example, if one is interested in producing some designer cookware and one has seen a sample, the 'essence' of which one would like to replicate, one could give a designer a general brief describing the type of cookware which was desired. For example, the brief could consist of 'white plates decorated with Italian food themes or landscapes'. Provided the designer has not seen the original, he/she is likely to come up with something similar in theme, but critically different from the point of view of copyright. This practice is sometimes used in the computer program design field to replicate functionality legally, but not copy any underlying code. The process is called 'clean room engineering'.

Despite the fact that copyright may not be infringed if time is taken to extract aspects of design that are unprotectable, and independent development is applied to those aspects, the rule against copying is nevertheless generally tougher than one might expect. The courts, particularly in the UK, are inclined to take the view that 'what is worth copying is worth protecting'. Where clear indicia of direct access to the original work, or 'the fingerprints' of copying exist, the courts are unlikely to hesitate in finding that an infringement has occurred.

2.2 WHAT IS PROTECTED BY COPYRIGHT AND HOW DOES COPYRIGHT ARISE?

Copyright in the UK exists by reason of a single statute: the Copyright Designs and Patents Act 1988.

Part I of this statute (admittedly regularly amended by 'statutory instrument') specifies precisely which works may be protected by copyright in the United Kingdom and what conditions there are, if any, for copyright protection.

If something does not fall squarely within the descriptions of what are classified as the 'copyright works' stated within the 1988 Act then it will not be protected as a copyright work. It may, however, be protected as another form of intellectual property (see section 2.1 above).

Example: Children's K'Nex Construction Kits are colourful, pleasing to use and well designed. However, as commercially produced objects, their shape and configuration are protected by another form of protection – design right rather than copyright. This expires sooner than copyright protection and the rules regarding reproduction and copying are different.

Current copyright law in the UK has developed piecemeal since the sixteenth century. Originally a form of protection and censorship (early control was vested in the notorious Star Chamber), copyright protection was first given to printed books and pamphlets. In turn, copyright status was extended, for instance, to cover engravings (from 1734), sculpture (from 1814), and other artistic works (from 1862).

The twentieth century has seen an extraordinary development in media – and there is a wide variety of works which now fall within the ambit of copyright protection: computer software is now bundled up with poetry and song lyrics – all as 'literary works'; the protection for photographs has led, in turn, to films, broadcasts and cable programmes also being protected as copyright works.

The following are identified as copyright works in the 1988 Act:

- Original literary, dramatic, musical or artistic works
- Sound recordings, films, broadcasts or cable programmes
- The typographical arrangements of published editions

These descriptions can be enlarged upon:

Literary works

These cover the written word: novels, poems, letters as well as manuals and other non-fiction works.

The definition expressly includes tables and compilations. Accordingly, listings, chronological tables, business literature, logarithm tables, television listings and schedules of stock exchange prices are all classified as literary works and therefore protected by copyright.

'Compilations' include compilations not only of other literary works (such as anthologies), but also sets of visual tables, diagrams and digests of news items. There can therefore be a compilation (a literary work) of photographs (which are artistic works: see below p. 14).

Song lyrics are also classified as literary works – but here there is an express exclusion of 'dramatic or musical works'. Those works are covered by copyright – but are classified under their own headings. There is no difference in protection; it is simply a question of categorisation.

Literary works mean anything which is written, spoken or sung. Accordingly, something written in shorthand or telegraph code could be a literary work; an extempore speech, for instance, could also be a literary work once it has been recorded in some form.

Can a single word be copyright protected? No: single invented words, even though original, cannot be literary works; nor can titles of magazines or books, nor advertising slogans.

Example: A group of museums wish to establish a joint trading subsidiary and a quarterly magazine both called 'Museums for the Millennium'. There is no copyright protection in that expression since such short expressions are not classified as 'literary works'. However, once the group had been trading for a while, they might be able to establish some reputation or goodwill in the name which could, possibly, be protected by another legal right: passing off. But there would be no copyright in the title.

Computer programs are expressly included in the 1988 Act as literary works.

The program need not be transcribed in a text which can be read in the normal way; it can be written in machine code or any programing language. It must, however, be recorded in some way, on, for example, CD-ROM, floppy disk, hard disk or, more simply, as a print out of the computer program.

Associated material for computer software (such as manuals, detailed instructions and preparatory design materials for computer programs) are also protected as copyright works.

Dramatic works

This category covers plays, dance, mime and other dramatic works provided that they are recorded in some way: this can be in writing, in Benesh notation or simply by recording the performance on video or tape.

There has been some discussion as to whether formats for TV shows like 'This is Your Life' and structures for sitcoms and game shows are dramatic works. Currently, such formats are not protected but the content of the individual programmes are.

Databases

Databases may have copyright protection. A database to which copyright protection can be given is defined as a collection of independent works, data or other materials which are arranged in a systematic or methodical way and are individually accessible by electronic or other means.

The database has to be an author's 'own intellectual creation'.

Example: A scholar creates a database of words from Shakespeare plays and identifies which of those had first been originated by William Shakespeare; the classification then shows the subsequent usage of those particular words in later manuscripts.

All the information is available to any researcher and indeed, in the public domain. The information will not be particularly original but, nevertheless, the database will be the scholar's own intellectual creation and therefore protected by copyright.

Note: even where the database is not an intellectual creation (and therefore not protected by copyright but is a more mundane collection of information), it may also be protected by a separate (more limited) right: the database right: see section 2.4.

Musical works

All types of music are covered. The music does not need to be written down as crotchets and quavers on a traditional five line stave – the work can simply be recorded, for instance, straight onto tape or through a keyboard. The lyrics for a song are classified separately as literary works: see above p. 13.

Artistic works

This is a wide-ranging category. It covers not only two-dimensional but also three-dimensional works. An artistic work includes:

- A painting
- A drawing
- A plan, map or chart
- Any form of engraving or print
- A collage
- A sculpture (and this includes anything chiselled, carved, modelled or cast)
- A photograph (both negative and final print) as well as a hologram
- An original design such as individual letters or typeface

Copyright protection is given to all the above irrespective of artistic merit; it is enough that the work is original.

Example: Each of a contemporary oil portrait, Carl Andre's Equivalent VIII (the Tate Gallery's pile of bricks) as well as a Japanese tourist's predictable photograph of Big Ben, will all have identical copyright protection as artistic works. Artistic merit is not relevant.

Works of architecture

These are also covered as artistic works. The protection is given to the buildings themselves as well as models for the buildings. Architects' plans, visualisations and sketches are protected, in any case, as drawings (the 1988 Act refers to 'graphic works').

The Courts give a wide interpretation to the meaning of 'building': this can include underground houses, as well as detailed internal features of the design of a particular building. Landscape gardens can also, in some circumstances, be protected as works of architecture.

Works of artistic craftsmanship

This is another impenetrable legal description for a certain type of artistic work.

The intention is that this particular category should cover works of applied art which do not fall under any of the other descriptions of artistic work. Works should have been 'crafted' in some way and in an 'artistic fashion'.

There is no further enlightenment within the 1988 Act about this peculiar category and, indeed, in one case (the only case) in the House of Lords, there were conflicting views as to what was meant by a work of artistic craftsmanship. The case concerned a rain cape designed for a mother and child.

By reason of this court decision and the fact that most clothes are principally defined by their function, it is possible that the shape and cut of many fashion garments are not protected by copyright; however, any surface decoration or textile design would probably be protected as an original artistic work.

It is probably only highly unusual haute couture designs which have genuine copyright protection for the full term of copyright.

Example: A student fashion designer includes in her end of year fashion show, a beautifully shaped Japanese jacket using a new textured print fabric also designed and printed by her. It is probable that the shape, cut, texture and unusual choice of fabrics and buttons would not be sufficient to give the garment itself any copyright protection. But, the design on the material will, if original, be protected by copyright as an artistic work.

Furniture

Most furniture is principally defined by functional aspects and, in many cases, will have been derived from earlier designs. Accordingly, much manufactured furniture will not be protected by copyright, but design right protection may still be available (see below).

Highly unusual one-off pieces may, however, be classified as sculpture or works of artistic craftsmanship and therefore protected by copyright.

Is artistic merit required? Although this category is described as 'artistic works', apart from works of artistic craftsmanship and architectural works, no artistic quality is required. Accordingly, extracts from A-Z street maps, computer generated graphs, seismic survey printouts can all be artistic works – even though the artwork can be utterly pedestrian. In short, the work does not need to be such that it would obviously be exhibited in an art gallery.

Example: A group of schoolchildren sit on the floor of a gallery making sketches of some of the artefacts on display. However accurate or inaccurate the results, the sketches will all be original artistic works – and therefore protected by copyright.

There is one exception: anything which is simply a slavish reproduction with no particular skill or labour involved may not have any copyright protection. There must be something more than what one judge described as 'trivial effort'.

Example: A museum publishes a facsimile edition of a book of previously published eighteenth-century engravings. The engravings are reproduced using an advanced photocopying machine and printed on good quality paper. It is unlikely that the engravings, as republished, would have any independent copyright since there is no originality in the final results.

However, where there is sufficient skill and labour, copyright protection can be given to duplicates. This is a highly contentious area and the question as to whether a picture library's stock of photography of fine art is protected by copyright has recently been the subject of litigation in the USA.

The leading UK textbook *Copinger & Skone James on Copyright* (14th edition) Sweet & Maxwell 1999, comments as follows:

> In relation to artistic works, a change of medium will often entitle a reproduction of an existing artistic work to independent protection. (An) example is an engraver who is almost invariably a copyist but his work may still be original in the sense that he has employed skill and judgment in its production. . . . The engraver produces his effect by the management of light and shade or, as the terms of his art expresses it, the chiaroscuro. The required degree of light and shade are produced by different lines and dots; the engraver must decide on the choice of the different lines or dots for himself, and on his choice depends the success of his print. A photographer who takes a picture of a work of art, such as a painting or a sculpture, may be treated as being in the same category, in that he may bring to the process of photographing the work, considerable skill as regards the angle from which to take the photograph, the lighting, the use of the right film and filter and so on.

Example: A gallery photographer takes careful colour controlled photographs of some of the canvasses on display. Careful light meter readings are taken and the lights are adjusted to prevent glare; Polaroid shots are also taken so that the photographer can use his or her judgment to check (and adjust) colour balance, glare and composition. The resulting transparencies, as photographs, may well be original artistic works and therefore protected by copyright.

Note: it is only the photographs themselves that would, by reason of the photography, be protected by copyright. The act of photographing another artistic work does not resurrect copyright in any way in old paintings in respect of which copyright may have expired: but see section 3.4: Publication right.

16

Example: A museum has a number of important (but battered) photographic images from the turn of the century. The museum takes pains in touching up cracks and redefining certain areas of the prints; because there has been some skill, labour and artistic judgment involved, the resulting photographic prints may be protected by copyright. Note, however, that in legal terms, there is still no decided position in this respect.

Such photography does not resurrect copyright in the old photograph which may or may not be protected by copyright. If copyright has expired in the old photograph, there can be no further restrictions on the copying of that photograph directly from the original or from old books or previously published material. Any new copyright which arises only relates to reproduction of the new original: but see section 3.4: Publication right.

Example: The same gallery photographer asks a technician to photograph a sheaf of old pen and ink drawings for record purposes. The technician uses an automatic overhead camera with a fixed range and with fixed lighting. It is probable that the resulting photographs would not be accorded copyright protection.

Sound recordings

A sound recording is any recording of sounds from which the sounds may be reproduced. This may cover such media as audio tapes, CD-ROMs, wax discs and microchips. The recordings do not need to have any originality; recordings of wildlife, traffic noise, people talking or steam engines will all be protected as copyright works as sound recordings.

Example: An enthusiast makes a recording of different aircraft noises. The resulting sound recording, although trite and with no artistic input from the maker of the sounds, will be protected as a copyright work.

It should be noted however that a duplicate copy of an existing sound recording is not, itself, a fresh copyright work; copyright cannot subsist in a sound recording to the extent that it is a copy taken from a previous sound recording.

Sound tracks of films are protected within the definition of films: see below.

Films

A 'film' is a recording on any medium from which a moving image may, by any means, be produced. Accordingly, the definition will cover film footage and video whether recorded in digital or analogue format. Sound tracks for films are also included within this definition.

Formerly, there was some doubt as to whether a single frame alone in a film could be as protected as a film; it had been argued that the single frame itself was not a 'sequence' of moving images and it therefore had no copyright protection. However, it has been held that a single frame of a film is, indeed, protectable as part of a film.

17

Example: An exhibition designer takes a photograph of a single frame from the film of 'A Room With A View'. The image is then blown up and used as a backdrop in an exhibition of women's fashions. The production company who own the copyright in the film could object to this unauthorised use of their copyright work.

Broadcasts

This covers both television broadcasts and sound broadcasts and covers any transmission by 'wireless telegraphy' including encrypted transmissions. Broadcasts also include certain satellite broadcasts.

Cable programme

This gives protection to any cable programme service other than by 'wireless telegraphy'.

Typographical arrangements of published editions

This is the form and layout of a typeset edition of any work – usually a book or periodical. Copyright protection is therefore given to publishers as well as the writers.

Example: A company publishes a new edition in a new format of Dante's Inferno together with a detailed introduction and explanatory footnote. The introduction and the explanatory footnotes will be an original literary work – the copyright of which will, typically, be owned by the author. The form and layout of the whole book will be a published edition – and accordingly, the publisher will have copyright in that typographical arrangement. The translator may also have a separate copyright.

The protection does not however apply to facsimile editions, apart from those elements of the edition which have been introduced by the new publisher.

What is not protected by copyright?

It is useful to indicate some of the items which would not be classified as copyright works:

- Ideas alone – those which are not reduced into any identifiable work
- Single invented words or short slogans
- Titles of books or magazines
- A 'slavish' copy of an original artistic work (for instance, a photocopy or straightforward photographic reproduction without any particular input from the operator/photographer)
- A duplicate of a sound recording

- Works which, on the grounds of public policy are not protected. (There have been cases concerning works which are libellous, immoral, obscene, scandalous or irreligious or which involve public deception.)

Note: This denial of copyright protection is rarely enforced. If the Courts found something wholly objectionable for these reasons, they would tend to deal with the matter by refusing to enforce the relevant copyrights rather than declaring that no copyright subsists in such works.

What about works which themselves infringe another copyright work? It had previously been considered that if a work itself infringed the copyright of another work then the new work could not have copyright protection. This is not currently the case. Even if a work infringes another work, then there can still be independent copyright protection.

Conditions for copyright protection

Like almost all laws, copyright law is domestic. In the UK, it principally serves to protect UK copyrights from infringement within the country. There are, however, qualification requirements for protection under UK law. This requires that, in order for a work which falls within one of the descriptions of copyright work to be protected within this country, there needs first to be some connection with the UK.

This is known as 'qualification' and is dependent on:

- the nationality;
- the domicile; or
- the residence, of the originator; or
- the place of first publication

It is not, however, only those persons closely connected with the UK who have copyright protection given to their original works. The UK is signatory to an international convention, the Berne Convention on the Protection of Artistic and Literary Works.

This major convention requires those countries which have signed the convention to give reciprocal protection, to certain minimum standards, to persons who are connected with any other country which is a signatory to the same convention.

The net effect of this is that, in accordance with its international obligations, the UK gives protection here, not only to persons who are nationals, residents or domiciliaries of the UK but also to persons who are nationals, residents or domiciliaries of any of the *other* convention countries. Additionally (or alternatively), protection is given here if any copyright work has first been published in any of those countries.

All developed nations are signatories to the Berne Convention and curators can readily assume that, in most instances, whether a work had been created by a UK national or a foreign national and/or whether it was first published here or abroad, it will have copyright protection within the UK.

19

Occasionally, there are instances of difficulty as in the case of countries which have divided and reformed (such as Germany after World War Two) or where existing boundaries alter (such as within the former Yugoslavia).

It should be reiterated that foreign copyrights do not require any special registration here in the UK; they are just as effective as UK copyrights and the same permissions would still need to be obtained for any relevant reproduction: see section 2.5 below.

2.3 HOW LONG DOES COPYRIGHT LAST?

The first point to establish is when the period of copyright protection begins. Copyright is normally held to begin when the copyright work is made. When does the law regard a work as having been made?

The textbooks refer to a work 'being reduced to a material form'; this means nothing more than writing something down, sketching out a picture or putting something onto tape. The work does not need to be in its final form and, even if it is edited, substantially changed or improved upon later, it still does not affect the copyright protection which is given to the original work.

Quite simply (apart from broadcasts or cable programmes) the copyright work must attach to a thing: whether it is a piece of paper, a computer disk or some magnetic tape. This is known as 'fixation'.

In the US, they use the expression 'to copyright' something. In Britain, not every noun can be 'verbed' as famously asserted by Sam Goldwyn – and indeed, something becomes copyright without any transitive action on the part of its originator, other than it coming into existence. No formalities are involved; no applications need be made for registration.

Until 1989, there was, in the US, a necessity for copyright works to be registered at the Library of Congress in Washington DC in order to obtain copyright protection; although this is still possible, and it does have some advantages (relating to remedies for copyright infringement), it is now not necessary even for US nationals.

Here in the UK, Stationers' Hall does have a facility to 'register' copyright – however, this is nothing more than a deposit of a copy of the original work; effectively, a receipt is given by them to confirm that they received the particular work on a particular day. The same can be done by lodging a copy of an original work with a friend, bank manager or solicitor or, indeed, sending something to oneself in a sealed envelope.

These actions do not create copyright; they simply recall (and, hopefully, prove) that on a particular date, a particular work was in existence. They do nothing more than that and, indeed, there is no greater need.

Example: A commuter creates on a scrap of paper the first few rough lines of a poem. Copyright protection is given immediately to that work – even in its unfinished form. On the same train, a designer visualises in his mind an idea for a new corporate logo for a multi-national client. No copyright protection is given until the designer reaches his agency and lays down a rough idea on paper.

Most books and many other copyright works carry the © symbol; many records, as well, contain ℗ . These symbols are simply a cautionary notice to the world that there is copyright in the relevant book or sound recording. It is useful practice but does not alter the fact that copyright will already have arisen.

Example: A catalogue written by an art historian is published by a gallery in conjunction with a show. Inadvertently, the copyright by-line (© plus the name of the author and the date of first publication) is not included in the proof and the catalogue is published without it. No harm is done. The author still has copyright and has all the rights available to a copyright owner under the 1988 Act.

How long does copyright last?

Copyright does not last forever. It 'subsists' and then expires. The period that copyright lasts for is called the 'term of copyright'.

When copyright has expired, it is said to be in the public domain – in other words, it can be freely used without restriction. The rationale is that an author 'should reap the profits of his own ingenuity and labour' and that it is in the interests of society that original works are created. The incentive given to the creator is that they obtain a form of monopoly, the exclusive right called copyright – but this is not forever: it is only for a limited period.

The earliest copyrights lasted only for 14 years with a possibility of a further 14-year extension. The term of copyright has been extended over time partly because the commercial interests of those industries (and countries) that depend on copyright have grown strongly but partly also because people are living longer. Recently, the term of copyright throughout European Union countries was extended, for most categories of copyright works, to life plus 70 years on the basis that this would, typically, cover the author and their two following generations. People have greater life expectancy than they had at the turn of the century when the copyright term was, for most categories of works, life plus 50 years.

The term of copyright has, over the last 300 years, fluctuated for different periods and for different categories of work. It may still be necessary to establish the copyright terms given by earlier copyright acts but this can be complicated; most copyright acts have 'transitional provisions' and the inter-play between these and the earlier copyright acts can tax the minds of even the most experienced copyright practitioners.

There is still relevance in working out the terms of copyright granted in the past. It may be relevant for a museum or gallery to consider an old work and ascertain whether copyright in the work might have expired. This can be relevant to publication right (see section 3.4: Publication right).

These are the terms of the copyright protection under the current law:

Works created after August 1989

Literary works	70 years from the end of the year in which the author died
Dramatic works	70 years from the end of the year in which the author died
Musical compositions	70 years from the end of the year in which the author died
Artistic works	70 years from the end of the year in which the author died
Sound recordings	50 years from the end of the calendar year in which it was made or 50 years from the date of release, whichever is the later
Broadcast and cable programmes	50 years from first broadcast or delivery
Typographical arrangements	25 years from the end of the year in which the edition was first published
Works of unknown authorship	70 years after the end of the calendar year in which the work is first made available to the public or 70 years from the date of making, whichever is the later
Works of joint authorship	70 years from the end of the calendar year in which the sole surviving author dies

Works created after 1957 but before August 1989

Literary/dramatic/musical works	Generally, 70 years from the end of the year in which the author died.

But in respect of unpublished literary, dramatic or musical works where, at the author's death, the work had not been:

- published
- performed in public
- broadcast
- recorded in a cable programme service, nor
- recorded and offered for sale to the public

then copyright expires on the earlier of:

1 70 years after the end of the year in which the first of such acts took place, and

2 31 December 2039.

Artistic works (other than engravings and photographs)	70 years from the end of the year in which the artist died
Engravings:	
published prior to 1 August 1989	70 years from the end of the year in which the author died or 50 years from the end of the year in which the engraving was first published, whichever is the later.
Engravings:	
unpublished as at 1 August 1989	50 years from 1 January 1990 or 70 years from the end of the year in which the author died, whichever is the later
Photographs	70 years from the end of the year in which the author (the photographer) died
Anonymous/Pseudonymous	Literary, dramatic, musical or artistic works (except photographs) made and published before 1 August 1989: 70 years from the end of the calendar year in which the works were first published.
	Made before 1 August 1989 but unpublished as at that date: until 31 December 2039 unless, prior to that date it is first made available to the public in which case the term is extended to 50 years from end of year of it being made available to the public.
	OR
	70 years from the date of making, whichever is the longer
	Note: If the identity of the author becomes known, then the standard rule of life plus 70 years will apply

Relevant factors to ascertain

In considering duration, it is useful to identify the following information:

- The relevant category of copyright work
- Whether it is a work of unknown authorship
- Who the author was
- When the author died
- When the work was first published or first made available to the public
- Whether the work could be subject to Crown copyright

Copyright expiry under earlier legislation

Although the rules for new works under the current regulations (as at 1999) are fairly clear, the various copyright acts since 1709 have all granted differing periods of protection.

For the most part, successive legislation has tended to increase the copyright terms. Accordingly, it cannot be assumed that copyright in works whose term has now expired will have expired under the same rules as those now current.

Example: Edouard Manet died in 1883. At that time, the copyright term for paintings and drawings was 7 years after the death of the author. Such copyright therefore expired in 1890 – even though, subsequently, in 1912 the copyright term was extended to 50 years after the death of the author.

Example: Pierre Bonnard died in 1947. He created lithographs which were published in 1895. At that time, under UK law, lithographs (which were classified as engravings even though not using an intaglio technique) had a copyright term which lasted for 28 years from publication. However, the term has been successively extended and is now 70 years from the end of the year in which the author died. The copyright in these lithographs therefore now expires at the end of 2017.

Example: The etcher Anders Zorn (1860–1920) made some etchings in 1895. Although at the time of their publication the copyright term was 28 years from publication, this term was later extended under the Copyright Act 1911 to 50 years after the end of the year in which he died, namely to 1970. All Zorn's published artwork is now in the public domain.

Example: In January 1999, Spanish police raided a house on the Costa del Sol and found during the course of the drugs raid unpublished original letters from Napoleon Bonaparte to his lover. If these letters were now to be published they would be protected by copyright for 70 years.

Example: 'Bleak House' by Charles Dickens was published in 1853 with original engraved illustrations by H. K. Browne. Dickens died in 1870. The copyright in the text, as a literary work, would at that time have expired in 1895 (42 years after publication). The copyright in the illustrations would have expired in 1881 (28 years after publication). The work is therefore wholly in the public domain.

Example: In 1927, a dusty croquet box, levered open at Malahide Castle in Dublin, was found to contain a bundle of manuscript papers. These were, in fact, original journals and letters of James Boswell, dating from the 1780s. 'The Boswell Papers' (as they became known) were subsequently published by Yale University Press. Because the letters were formerly unpublished, they had remained in copyright. The effect of the publication gave an extended copyright protection until the 1970s, almost 200 years since they had first been written.

Duration of Crown copyright

The rules for this are beyond the scope of this book and depend on whether

- The work was made before or after 1 August 1989
- When the work was first published commercially
- Whether, if a photograph, it was taken before 1 June 1957

Generally, the relevant term for Crown copyright does not relate to the identity of, or date of death of, the author and can continue for a period of up to 125 years.

Joint ownership

Where there are two or more joint copyright owners, the copyright term is based on the date of death of the last of the copyright owners to die.

Example: John Lennon died in 1980; the copyright term in Lennon/McCartney compositions still continues and will last until 70 years after the end of the year in which Paul McCartney dies.

Can copyright be extended?

Between 1842 and 1912, the period of protection for published literary, dramatic and musical works was the author's life plus seven years or 42 years after publication, whichever was longer.

However, when the Copyright Act 1911 came into force, an extended term was substituted. If an original work was still in copyright at that time then a new term was substituted, namely, author's lifetime plus 50 years.

These extensions raised two questions: Did the new (extended) term apply to works originated before the date of the change – or just to new works created after that date? What was the position if the copyright in an older work had expired under the provisions of the old law – but would not have done if the new term of copyright was applied retroactively? In other words, could the copyright in old expired works be resurrected?

These questions were of little commercial significance at the turn of the century. However, the position at the end of the twentieth century is very different. Most copyrights could be exploited far more significantly and some copyrights were extremely valuable. The position became a matter of serious concern when the term of many copyrights was radically changed pursuant to a 1993 EU Directive. This is colloquially called 'the Term Directive' since it makes substantial changes to the term of copyright.

The background was as follows: As part of the European Commission's determination that there should be a level playing field across Europe and that, they deduced, copyright periods should be uniform throughout the European Union countries, the proposal was that the copyright term be 'harmonised'.

Of course, the European Commission had a choice – they could either harmonise down to the lowest period of copyright protection or they could choose the highest period. They chose the latter. The Commission's view was that authors' rights were important and that, in general, copyright protection should be increased rather than diminished. After considerable deliberation, the Term Directive was issued in October 1993.

For the principal categories of copyright works (artistic/literary/dramatic/ musical) the UK was required to conform to the requirements of the directive and to initiate domestic legislation to increase the term of copyright, here, to a uniform period of the author's life plus 70 years.

For new works, the situation was clear. They were to receive the new (enlarged) terms. Additionally, for works which were still in copyright, as in the case of the writer or artist dying within the preceding 50 years, then, when the new legislation finally came into effect (on 1 December 1995) the owners of the copyright in those works were automatically granted the extended period. The copyright term simply increased and the expiry date was postponed for a further 20 years.

Where copyright, therefore, was already in force in the UK there was an extension of copyright, the additional term being called 'extended copyright'. However, there was a complication: some works had fallen out of copyright. They were in the public domain. The works were past their 'sell-by' date and, for commercial purposes, were defunct – but they would, otherwise, have still have fallen within the life plus 70 years period that the European Commission was requiring across the EU.

What was to be done? Were the recently expired copyrights allowed to lay fallow or were they to be resurrected? The answer was that they were to be revived – on the basis that it was unfair and unequal treatment for a UK national having a copyright in a work in the UK to be treated less favourably to, say, a German national with an equivalent copyright work which remained in copyright in Germany.

Example: Virginia Woolf committed suicide in 1941. The copyrights in 'To the Lighthouse' therefore expired at the end of 1991. When the new rules came into effect, copyright in this revived and will now expire at the end of 2011.

Accordingly, the works were dusted down by their surprised owners and revived. This additional period of copyright protection is called 'revived copyright'.

Example: Beatrix Potter died in 1940; under the former rules, the copyright in both her text and her illustrations lapsed on 31 December 1990. Under the new rules, the copyrights were revived with effect from 1 December 1995 and royalties, again, had to be paid for the reproduction or use of the work. The owners of the rights, Frederick Warne & Co., obtained revived copyright.

There had to be special transitional provisions so that if someone took legitimate commercial steps to exploit something that was out of copyright during the intervening period, then they would not be prejudiced.

Example: A major publishing company signs a contract with an academic for a revised edition of 'Ulysses' by James Joyce in 1994. At that time, the works of James Joyce were out of copyright in the UK. The subsequent revival of the copyright in James Joyce's work does not affect the legitimacy of the contract.

Crown copyright

Where a work is made by Her Majesty or by an officer or servant of the Crown in the course of his duties, Crown copyright will subsist. The copyright is not of a different nature from the copyright which subsists in relation to other copyright works (books, plays, paintings, sound recordings, etc.) but there are two important differences from the normal rules. The first owner of copyright will be the Crown and the period that the copyright lasts, the term, differs from the usual rules.

What does Crown copyright cover?

- works made by Her Majesty or by an officer or servant of the Crown *in the course of his duties*
- work created by Civil Servants
- works of war artists or designated war photographers employed by the Crown

Crown copyright does not extend to BBC programmes, reports of Parliamentary debates, reports of Royal Commissions, Ordnance Survey maps or internal ministerial memos.

Crown copyright however specifically extends to:

- Acts of Parliament and
- measures of the General Synod of the Church of England

The Crown also has a bundle of separate rights similar to copyright called 'Crown prerogative'. The Crown has exclusive rights for the printing of:

- the King James translation of the Bible
- the 1662 Book of Common Prayer, and
- some law reports

Parliamentary copyright

Before 1989, the Crown was the first publisher (thereby the first owner of copyright) in reports of the proceedings of either of the Houses of Parliament and also Parliamentary bills. The position is slightly different now: bills and the reports are published by or under the direction or control of either the

House of Lords or House of Commons who, themselves, now become the copyright owners.

Note: Copyright in Parliamentary bills ceases within a short period – namely when the bill:

- either receives royal assent or

- at the end of the Parliamentary session, it is abandoned

The daily reports of Hansard are owned by the two Houses jointly. If a member of Parliament makes a speech in either House, then the copyright in that speech will be that of the member or peer as a literary work – but the copyright in the sound recording or Hansard report of that speech will be that of the relevant House.

Universities of Oxford and Cambridge

The two universities claim, alongside the Crown, to have the sole rights to publish the Authorised version of the Bible and the Book of Common Prayer.

Publication right

It used to be a ready assumption that once copyright had expired, free use could be made of the relevant material. The effect of the EU Directive on the term of copyright has already thrown this into disarray by either extending or reviving copyright in formerly out of copyright material (see section 3.4).

Publication right also changes the landscape. This gives, effectively, a fresh form of copyright (but without the 'moral' rights) for a period of 25 years if a work which is out of copyright but unpublished is then published.

This is of great importance to museums, many of which hold archives and collections of old material which may well fall into this category (see section 3.4).

2.4 OWNERSHIP OF COPYRIGHT AND HOW IT CAN BE TRANSFERRED

Creation of copyright works

Authorship and ownership – the concept of the 'first owner'

As explained in section 2.1 the concept of creation is central to the ownership of copyright. Copyright arises automatically, from the moment that an original work is created. It is a right which rewards the creation of such original works.

Copyright legislation designates the creator of a copyright work as its 'author' (regardless of the type of work created). It follows logically that the *first* owner of the copyright in an original work should be the author of it. This is the general rule. The writer of text, the painter of a painting, the taker of a photograph – these are 'authors' who will own the copyright in their work. The law uses the

28

term 'first' owner because, as we will see below, ownership can be assigned or transferred by this first owner to someone else, who then becomes a subsequent owner of the copyright.

There are some kinds of material however where the identity of the 'author' is not so clear, for example films, sound recordings and broadcasts. In these cases, the general rule defines the owner of copyright differently.

In the case of films, the producer and the principal director are deemed to be the 'authors' of a film and therefore the owners of the copyright in it. However, there are exceptions to this:

1   films made before 1 July 1994; under the law in force at that time the person who undertook the necessary arrangements for the making of the film (i.e. the producer) was the sole author and thus the sole owner of copyright;

2   copyright in other countries, whose laws may recognise a wider class of 'authors' of a film (e.g. the author of the screenplay, the composer of the music specifically composed for the film as well as the principal director).

The author of a sound recording is the producer of the recording and this person is therefore also the first owner of copyright in the sound recording.

The rules governing ownership of copyright in broadcasts and cable programmes are different again but are of less relevance to museums and galleries. Essentially it is the broadcaster who is regarded as the author of the broadcast and hence the first owner of copyright in it.

Multiple authorship

Clearly, there are many examples of works where there may be more than one 'author'. Books to which several authors have contributed are one example; films another, where, as stated above, the law (in the UK at least) explicitly recognises that there are two persons who share in the authorship of a film, the producer and the principal director.

In some of these cases, it will be possible to distinguish the contributions of the respective authors. Each author would therefore begin by owning the copyright to his or her contribution. There are cases, however, where the collaboration between two or more authors is so close that their respective contributions cannot be distinguished. Where the contribution of one author to a work is 'not distinct' from that of another, the law recognises a situation of joint authorship. In these circumstances, the copyright in the work is jointly owned by the joint authors. This has some important consequences for the way in which the ownership of copyright is treated.

Depending on the relationship between the joint authors, the law recognises two forms of joint ownership – a 'joint tenancy' and a 'tenancy in common'. The principal difference between these two forms of joint ownership is that, in the case of a 'joint tenancy', on the death of the one joint owner, his copyright will pass to the other joint owner, whereas in the case of a 'tenancy in common', on the death of the one joint owner, his copyright will pass under his will or otherwise to his next of kin. This is a complex area on which advice should be sought.

A more important consequence of joint ownership is that no one can safely acquire an exclusive licence from one of the joint owners, because the other joint owner may be freely granting licences under the same (jointly owned) copyright. Anyone wishing to buy the copyright or to acquire an exclusive licence under it must therefore make sure that both (or if there are more than two, all) joint owners sign the assignment or exclusive licence.

Of course, the same is true of multiple ownership where no question of joint ownership, in the strict legal sense, arises. If all the rights in a work of multiple ownership are required then all the owners should be identified and should sign any document dealing in those rights.

Employees' works

As explained, the general rule is that the first owner of copyright in a copyright work is the author of that work.

Where however the author is an *employee* who has made a work in the course of his/her employment, then it is the *employer* who is the 'first owner' of the copyright in the employee's work. This is consistent with the general principle that the product of an employee's work belongs to his employer, in return for which the employee is paid.

It is vital to appreciate that an employee in this case is someone employed under a contract of service, i.e. someone under the overall direction and control of his employer, whose equipment may be supplied by his employer and whose employer will, in many cases, be paying his/her salary on a PAYE basis. Freelances who are responsible for their own tax and who supply their own equipment or tools are *not* employees.

This means that where an individual is engaged to create a work (write text, design a gallery, take photographs) on a one-off basis, or on terms that that individual is responsible for his/her own income tax, then the person engaging him/her will not automatically own the copyright in the resulting work. Ownership will need to be transferred to the commissioning party by means of an assignment (see below, p. 32).

A very common example of such a situation is where photographs are commissioned; this can be contrasted with the position where they are taken by an employed staff photographer. In the former case, the first owner of the copyright in the photographs is the photographer (the 'author'). In the second, it is the employer, because the photographs were taken by the photographer in the course of his employment.

The general rule, in the case of works created by employees in the course of their employment (i.e. that the copyright in such works belongs to the employer), is subject to agreement to the contrary. Such agreements to the contrary are unusual. For the general rule to be set aside, they would need either:

1   to be expressly reflected in the contract of employment; or

2   to be clearly reflected in some generally accepted course of dealing in a given sector.

An example of 2 is the academic world where, traditionally at least, university employed academics are treated as owning the copyright in their writings (including lectures) even if, strictly, writing and delivering lectures is one of the things they are employed to do. This situation has applied in the past in the case of some museums, where the copyright in at least some works created by curators has been treated as belonging to the curators. This situation is, however, changing as museums become more dependent on self-generated income streams to support their activities (and indeed pay curators' salaries).

Crown copyright

Crown copyright is a category of copyright peculiar to UK law. It is a form of copyright which protects works created by Her Majesty or by an officer or servant of the Crown in the course of his duties. Before 1989, it applied to works created by someone working under the direction or control of Her Majesty or a government department.

The relevance of Crown copyright to museums is twofold:

1 Some museums may contain holdings of Crown copyright material as part of their collections (for example, the war footage held in the collections of the Imperial War Museum).

2 The status of some museums was such that, until recently, their staff were deemed to be officers or servants of the Crown, and so any works created by them in the course of their duties would have been Crown copyright. This was the case with those museums whose status was regulated by the National Heritage Act 1983 and the Museums and Galleries Act 1992.

Crown copyright is dealt with by the Controller of Her Majesty's Stationery Office under Royal Letters Patent. A museum wishing to obtain the right to exploit the Crown copyright in works falling into the categories mentioned above should obtain a 'delegated authority' from the Controller unless such exploitation falls within one of the permitted classes. The regime governing the management of Crown copyright will change following the Government's White Paper *The Future Management of Crown Copyright* (Cm 4300).

Revived and extended copyrights

As explained in section 2.3, in 1995 the UK implemented an EC Directive extending the period of copyright protection in the case of literary, dramatic, musical and artistic works from the life of the author plus 50 years to the life of the author plus 70 years. One consequence was the 'revival' of copyright in older works, the copyright in which had previously expired. This revived copyright is owned by the same person as owned the copyright immediately before it expired. However, if that person had died (or in the case of a company, ceased to exist) before 1 January 1996, then the revived copyright belongs to the author of the work concerned or his personal representatives or in the case of a film, its principal director or his personal representatives.

In the case of copyrights still unexpired when these new provisions came into force ('extended copyrights'), the extended copyright belongs to the person who owned the copyright immediately before the extension came into force (i.e. 1 January 1996).

Overseas works

Because the United Kingdom is a signatory to the principal international conventions dealing with copyright (the Berne Convention and the Universal Copyright Convention), its copyright law confers on most overseas nationals the same protection for their works as is conferred in the UK on UK nationals. However, the rules of ownership of copyright are not harmonised internationally. This means that the copyright in any work of overseas origin may well be owned according to principles which differ from those set out in this chapter, and advice may need to be sought. Generally speaking, however, most countries recognise the author as the 'first' owner of copyright.

Transmission and licensing of copyright

Generally   Being able to trace how the ownership of copyright may have been transmitted is of vital importance, particularly, in the case of museums, in relation to exploiting older copyright works (for example those in a museum's collections). The complexities of such investigations are dealt with in chapter 3, especially sections 3.2 and 3.4.

There are a number of ways in which copyright may be transmitted. It can be assigned in a number of ways or, on the death of a copyright owner, can be dealt with in the owner's will or otherwise pass to his next of kin.

Assignment of copyright   The ownership of copyright may be transferred from one person to another. This operation is known as an 'assignment'. To be effective, an assignment must:

1   be in writing; and
2   the document containing the assignment must be signed by the person assigning the copyright. The document must clearly state that copyright is being assigned. Otherwise, there is no special requirement as to the form of the document.

Since copyright can be sub-divided into a number of component parts, namely the different rights 'bundled' together into the totality of the copyright in a work (the right to reproduce, the right to translate etc.), the territories in which it may be exploited and even the period of exploitation, the law does permit 'partial' assignments of copyright. So, for example, a copyright owner can assign some but not all of the rights in the bundle (e.g. the right to reproduce in books but not in CD-ROMs). He can also assign these rights for some but not all of the copyright period. He can assign these rights in some countries, but not others.

Because copyright is a concept that can be abstracted from the physical material in which it arises (see section 2.1), it is possible to assign copyright before the work in which it arises has come into existence. This is described as an assignment by a 'prospective owner' of a 'future copyright'. It is commonly found in situations where party A commissions party B to create a work, as a term of which party B assigns the future copyright in the (not yet created) commissioned work to party A.

Unpublished works bequeathed by will Where a document containing an unpublished literary, dramatic, musical or artistic work or an original recording of sound or film is left by will, and the testator was entitled to the copyright in the work or record, then unless the copyright is specifically mentioned, it is deemed to pass to the same person as is entitled to the bequest of the document or record. This rule does not apply to published works (where the original document or record may no longer exist).

Licensing A copyright owner can permit or authorise someone else to do something which is otherwise restricted by copyright. Such a permission or authorisation is called a licence. Licensing copyrights lies at the heart of many forms of copyright exploitation, such as publishing or merchandising.

A licence may be *exclusive*, in which case the licensee is the only person entitled to do what is permitted under the copyright licence – even the copyright owner gives up the right to do such acts. To be effective, exclusive licences must be in writing, and they must be signed by the copyright owner. These formalities, it will be noted, are similar to those required for assignments (see above). This is because they both serve to confer the exclusive rights of the copyright owner on another person (although in the case of the assignment, this is achieved by a complete transfer of the ownership of the copyright).

Where the copyright owner permits more than one person to do certain things otherwise restricted by the copyright, then those persons have '*non-exclusive* licences'. Non-exclusive licences do not require any formalities to be effective, but their duration and enforceability may depend on whether they are granted as part of a contract (see section 2.5).

Licences, whether exclusive or non-exclusive, may be granted subject to conditions. Indeed, it is very common – and indeed advisable from the copyright owner's perspective – for licences to be granted as part of a contract under which the licensee pays a licence fee or royalty, and accepts certain conditions and obligations in return for the licence. These reflect the fact that a copyright owner will usually wish to exert some continuing control over the activities of a licensee to prevent the value of the copyright from being undermined.

At the same time, the licensee will naturally wish to be satisfied that the rights granted are the owner's to grant, and that they have not previously been dealt with in any way which would affect the licensee's rights under the licence. The licensee will therefore seek warranties to this effect from the owner (see section 3.2).

A licensee may be permitted to sub-license the rights further to third parties. There is no reason in principle why copyright should not be sub-licensed and sub-sub-licensed in this way *ad infinitum*, but it is rare where a copyright owner is anxious to preserve control over the way in which the copyright is exploited.

Databases

Databases may be protected by copyright or by 'database right' (a database can only be protected by copyright if the selection or arrangement of the contents is the author's own intellectual creation). It is important to note that the rules regarding ownership of these rights are different. So far as any *copyright* in a database is concerned, this is owned according to the rules set out in this chapter. *Database right*, however, is dealt with differently. The 'maker' of a database is the person who takes the initiative in obtaining, verifying or presenting the contents of the database, and bears the cost of doing so. This may very well be a different person from the actual compiler. It is this person who is the first owner of the database right.

An example of this may be when a museum commissions a freelance person to design a database for the museum (e.g. a collections database). If the way in which the contents of the database are selected and arranged is intellectually original, then the freelance person will own *copyright* in the database (unless he/she assigns it to the museum as part of the commissioning contract).

However, the museum is likely to be deemed to be the person who takes the initiative and bears the cost of building the database, so it is the museum which will own the *database right* in it.

However, where a database is made by an employee in the course of his duties (for what is meant by an 'employee', see above), the maker, and therefore first owner of the database right in the database is deemed to be the employer.

Database right may be assigned and licensed in a similar manner to copyright.

Moral rights

The various rights known as 'moral rights' (the right to be identified as author, the right to object to derogatory treatment of one's work, the right not to have a work falsely attributed to one and the right to privacy of privately commissioned photographs or films), though they may all be waived, *cannot* be assigned. They all remain vested in the author because they are intrinsically bound up with the author's reputation and person.

Therefore the right to exercise the moral rights of the author may very well belong to someone other than the copyright owner.

An author may however bequeath the right to exercise his moral rights after his death to someone. If there is no such direction in his will then the right to exercise the moral rights will pass to the same person who becomes the copyright owner. However, if there is no person to whom the author's copyright passes (for example, because he assigned the copyright to someone else before his death), then the right to exercise his moral rights passes to his personal representatives (i.e. his executors or the administrators of his estate).

2.5 USE AND ABUSE OF COPYRIGHT

Unauthorised use of copyright works

Acts restricted by copyright

Copyright law speaks of those 'acts which are restricted by copyright': these are the things that a copyright owner has the exclusive right to do (or to permit others to do) with his work. They are:

1 copying the work (the right of reproduction);

2 issuing copies to the public (the right of distribution);

3 renting or lending of copies of the work to the public;

4 performing, playing or showing the work in public;

5 broadcasting the work or including it in a cable programme service; and

6 adapting the work.

If any of these things are done without the authority of the copyright owner, then the copyright is infringed, and the owner is entitled to various remedies to compensate the owner for the infringement (see section 2.5: Consequences of unauthorised use). The doing of any of these things to the whole *or* a substantial part of a work is restricted. 'Substantial' is interpreted both qualitatively and quantitatively. This means that the significance of the part in question will be assessed. The mere fact that the part copied is only a small fraction of the whole may not mean that there is no infringement. Reproducing a sonnet may still infringe even though it is only fourteen lines long.

It is also very important to appreciate that *authorising* someone else to commit an infringement is itself an infringement. For example, in a contract commissioning a design, imposing a term that the design should resemble another design might well amount to authorising the designer to infringe copyright in the other design.

Copying

Copying includes storing a work in any medium by electronic means. This means that *scanning* a copyright work will result in an infringing copy unless authorised. It also means that, in relation to computer programs, merely running them (which results in a copy being made) is an infringement unless authorised.

Issuing copies to the public

This means putting copies of a work into circulation that have not previously been put into circulation. In other words, once the making and distribution of certain copies has been authorised, their *subsequent* circulation (e.g. sale by a wholesaler to retailer or retailer to members of the public) cannot be prevented.

Renting or lending of copies of the work to the public

Renting or lending of copies of the work to the public infringes the copyright in the work unless authorised by the copyright owner. 'Rental' means making a copy of a work available on terms that it will or may be returned, for direct or indirect commercial advantage. It therefore includes such activities as video rental. 'Lending' means making a copy of a work available on terms that it will or may be returned, otherwise than for direct or indirect commercial advantage, through an establishment accessible to the public (e.g. a museum or a library). This is therefore primarily concerned with the activities of such bodies as public libraries, but will include, for example, the lending of photographic transparencies of copyright works (e.g. paintings).

Where a charge is made by an establishment accessible to the public, the lending remains lending if the charge does not go beyond what is necessary to cover the operating costs of the establishment, which means that lending between establishments accessible to the public is not an infringement of copyright.

Performing, playing or showing the work in public

Performing a literary, dramatic or musical (but not artistic) work in public infringes copyright in such a work unless authorised. 'Performance' includes delivery in the case of lectures or speeches, and in general includes any mode of visual or acoustic presentation.

Playing or showing a sound recording, film, broadcast or cable programme in public infringes the copyright in such a work unless authorised.

Broadcasting a work or including it in a cable programme service

The law makes clear that broadcasting a literary, dramatic, musical or artistic work, a sound recording or film, or another broadcast or cable programme, or including any of these in a cable programme service, infringes the copyright in such a work unless authorised.

Internet transmissions are not included. However, an international copyright treaty (the WIPO Copyright Treaty adopted in Geneva at the end of 1996) contains a provision giving to copyright owners 'an exclusive right to authorise or prohibit any communication to the public of originals or copies of their works, by wire or wireless means, including the making available to the public of their works in such a way that members of the public may access them from a place and at a time individually chosen by them'. This is intended to make Internet use an infringement if not authorised. A draft European Directive, which incorporates this provision, is currently under discussion and is likely to become law in the near future.

Adaptations

Adaptations of only certain types of work need the permission of the copyright owner: these are literary, dramatic and musical works. The principal forms of adaptation are translation and stage dramatisation of non-dramatic works (and vice versa).

'Secondary' infringement of copyright

The acts mentioned above are all 'primary' infringements. The copyright owner does not need to prove that the person doing them intended to infringe copyright or even knew that he was infringing copyright. Ignorance of the very existence of a copyright is therefore no defence to a claim of infringement. However, a primary infringement involves the doing of some act.

It is also possible to infringe copyright without doing anything. For example, it is possible to infringe simply by possessing copies in the course of a business, knowing or having reason to believe that the copies are infringing copies. Such an infringement is termed a 'secondary' infringement, because it is necessary to prove that the guilty party knew or had reason to believe that he was dealing with infringing copies. Other examples of secondary infringements are:

1 selling, offering for sale, exhibiting to the public in the course of a business or distributing copies of a work, knowing or having reason to believe that they are infringing copies;

2 where an occupier of premises gives permission for apparatus to be brought onto the premises, knowing or having reason to believe that the apparatus was likely to be used so as to infringe copyright (e.g. by an unauthorised playing or showing of a copyright work).

Criminal offences

Except in the world of counterfeiting, it is often ignored that certain unauthorised dealings with copyright works are criminal offences. Yet the criminal law does indeed buttress the rights of the copyright owner, seeing in unrestrained piracy a wrong which it is as much in the public interest to prevent as it is in the private interest of the copyright owner to restrain. Often the commission of a secondary infringement, which would entitle the copyright owner to bring civil proceedings for infringement, also entails the commission of a criminal offence for which the guilty party can be prosecuted.

Examples of such criminal offences are:

1 possessing in the course of a business with a view to committing any infringement of copyright, or

2 in the course of a business selling, offering for sale, exhibiting to the public or distributing

an article which the person concerned knows or has reason to believe is an infringing copy of a copyright work. Other offences deal with knowingly causing copyright to be infringed by means of an unauthorised public performance of a literary, dramatic or musical work or the unauthorised playing or showing in public of a sound recording or film. They are concerned primarily with piracy and counterfeiting. Enforcement is typically in the hands of local Trading Standards Officers or the relevant enforcement body.

Consequences of unauthorised use

Civil proceedings instituted by the copyright owner

The law provides to an owner of a copyright which has been infringed a battery of remedies which are intended to compensate the owner and ensure that the infringement does not happen again. The circumstances in which these remedies may be available are complicated and advice should always be obtained if any remedies need to be sought.

In broad terms a copyright owner has the following remedies, not all of them necessarily available concurrently:

1 damages, to compensate him for the loss occasioned by the unauthorised use of his work;

2 an account of the profits made by the infringer out of the unauthorised use;

3 an injunction preventing further unauthorised use;

4 an order for delivery up of infringing copies in the possession of a third party, for forfeiture to the copyright owner or destruction;

5 a right to seize infringing copies exposed for sale or hire.

In certain circumstances, where an infringement has only just come to light and it is vital to prevent the infringement from continuing, the courts will grant an interlocutory injunction. In appropriate situations this can be obtained within days or even hours and is an extremely valuable weapon for the copyright owner. Interlocutory injunctions are not granted, however, where the copyright owner has failed to act promptly.

Criminal proceedings

As indicated above, local Trading Standards Officers (in fact the local weights and measures authorities) typically enforce the criminal provisions of copyright law, with powers to make test purchases, seize goods and so on. Infringing goods are liable to be forfeited to the copyright owner or destroyed or otherwise dealt with as the court sees fit.

Authorised use of copyright works

Permission granted by the copyright owner

As we have seen, a copyright owner can permit or authorise someone else to do something which is otherwise restricted by copyright (see 'Licensing' in section 2.4). Such licences can be contractual, in which case the permission to exploit the copyright work is given in exchange for royalties and/or undertakings. Sometimes they are implied from the circumstances. In a situation where it is clear that a copyright owner has tolerated use of his copyright work without requiring an express licence, then a licence will be implied. However, the terms of an implied licence may be unclear. For example, it may not be obvious for how long such a licence should last. From the perspective both of the copyright owner and the licensee, it is therefore usually better to agree terms which can be expressly recorded. One of the purposes of standard terms and *pro forma* documents (such as those in section 4.2) is to achieve this objective.

Collective licensing

The copyright owner can delegate the task of granting permission to a third party. Various kinds of exploitation of copyright works are now subject to collective licensing schemes. These are schemes regulated under the Copyright, Designs and Patents Act 1988, under which copyright owners have delegated the licensing of particular activities to a collecting society. There are a number of these, administering copyright and rights in performances in different areas. The Copyright Licensing Agency Limited publishes a pocket directory of the societies administering these schemes. Examples of such societies are the following (their addresses and telephone numbers are set out in Appendix 4.2):

1 The Copyright Licensing Agency Limited (CLA)   The CLA is a joint collecting agency set up by Publishers Licensing Society Limited and Authors Lending and Copyright Society Limited (ALCS). Its purpose is to collect and share revenue from licences granted for the right to copy books and periodicals on reprographic machines (photocopiers). Standard licences have been developed and issued in the educational and commercial fields. The CLA has developed a protocol to its licence for higher education institutions for museums.

2 The Newspaper Licensing Agency Limited (NLA)   The NLA was established in 1996 as the collecting society for national newspapers. Its purpose is to license the rights that the publishers have in respect of the photocopying of cuttings taken from national newspapers.

3 The Performing Rights Society Limited (PRS)   The PRS administers the performing, broadcasting and cable programme rights in music on behalf of music publishers and composers. It should be noted that the PRS does not administer the rights in sound recordings (as distinct from the copyright in the music and lyrics), which are handled by PPL (see below).

4 Phonographic Performance Limited (PPL)   This organisation grants copyright licences for the public performance, broadcasting and distribution of sound recordings. It therefore represents the copyright interests of the recording companies rather than the artists themselves. Thus, if a museum were playing music it would need a licence from PPL to cover the recording company's interests and a licence from the PRS to cover the artists' interests.

5 Mechanical Copyright Protection Society (MCPS)   The MCPS represents publishers and composers of music and administers the collection and distribution of royalties due whenever musical works are recorded. It therefore collects royalties from recording companies and shares them out among music publishers and composers.

6 The Design and Artists' Copyright Society Limited (DACS)   DACS represents artists, photographers and their estates. It licenses the reproduction of artistic works in any medium. It has recently developed jointly with the CLA a licence covering photocopying of images.

39

In any case where reproduction of a copyright work might be licensed by one of these collecting societies, care needs to be taken to establish that the collecting society is entitled to handle the rights. The blanket licences offered by some of these collecting societies are intended to operate as a form of insurance against claims but the terms need to be carefully examined and can on occasion be negotiated. Disputes concerning such licences can be referred to the Copyright Tribunal, which has power to confirm or vary the scheme administered by a collecting society, including the terms of the licences granted, and to make a determination as to the reasonableness of the scheme or the terms of the licence.

Although the MCPS and PRS have formed a joint venture to deal with licences for multimedia exploitation, there is as yet no one-stop shop in the UK covering multimedia licences. Individual right holders and collecting societies in particular sectors still need to be approached. There are various initiatives looking at multimedia exploitation, notably IMPRIMATUR, an EU-funded project aiming to devise processes marrying technical and legal strategies to protect and license intellectual property rights (further details can be obtained on their web site: imprimatur@alcs.co.uk).

One of the most potentially interesting initiatives is the SCRAN (Scottish Cultural Resources Access Network) project, funded in part from lottery funds disbursed by the Millennium Fund, one of the distributing bodies of the UK National Lottery (more information can be obtained by accessing SCRAN's web site, which is at scran.ac.uk). This involves the digitisation of images of around 30,000 objects in the collections of museums and galleries across Scotland. The digitised images form part of a database combined with 1.5 million text records, data, captions and multimedia essays. The images are available at three levels. Thumbnail images are available for free via the Internet. Educational licences are made available for a fee, and finally very high quality digital images are available for commercial exploitation. However, apart from SCRAN there is nothing in the museum sector in the UK like the Museum Educational Site Licensing (MESL) project in the US.

The 'permitted acts'

Most systems of copyright law recognise limits to the scope of copyright protection by permitting certain things to be done without infringing copyright, where a less restrictive regime is deemed socially or culturally beneficial.

UK law is similar and provides for a number of exceptions that may be relevant to the use and exploitation by museums and galleries of copyright works:

1 Research or private study 'Fair dealing' with a copyright work for the purposes of research or private study does not infringe the copyright in the work. 'Fair dealing' means that the amount copied must be fair. The making available of a single digital image by a museum to a researcher or for solely private use would come within the exemption. The making available of multiple copies, however, would not. Research currently includes commercial research. It is not clear whether putting thumbnail images on a web site could ever fall within the exemption even if the site contained express statements that viewing or downloading was only permitted for

certain purposes because putting a digital file onto a web site might be regarded as tantamount to authorising multiple copying.

2 Criticism or review   'Fair dealing' with a copyright work for the purposes of criticism or review of that *or another* work does not infringe the copyright in the work, provided that the author of the work (not the copyright owner) is identified. In the case of a digital image of a painting in a museum collection, two authors might therefore need to be identified, namely the artist (if the painting itself remained in copyright) and the photographer (although since the latter is usually never identified when the photograph is published identifying the photographer would usually not be required). There is little guidance from reported cases on the scope of this exemption. Bona fide criticism rather than merely cursory comment in relation to a work is likely to be required by a court so that, for example, coffee table art books with little real critical content ought not to benefit from the exemption.

3 Education   Schools and colleges can copy works 'in the course of instruction or of preparation for instruction' so long as this is done in a classroom context; but museums and galleries will not qualify as they are not 'educational establishments'. However, database right in a database made available to the public is not infringed by fair dealing with a substantial part of its contents if it is extracted for the purpose of illustration for teaching or research and not for any commercial purpose. This is wider in some respects than the equivalent provisions applying to copyright. A museum might be able to rely on this exemption if, for example, it used a portion of a published image database in the course of educational and non-commercial activities within the museum. However, the copyrights in the individual images would still have to be cleared.

4 Libraries and archives   Prescribed libraries, that is, mainly public libraries – including the libraries maintained by museums and galleries – can (for example) supply single copies of articles in periodicals or single copies of extracts from books, so long as the copy is required for research and private study. They may also supply copies of works to other prescribed libraries.

5 Anonymous works   If it is not possible by reasonable enquiry to ascertain the identity of the author of a literary, dramatic, musical or artistic work, and it is reasonable to assume that copyright in the work has expired or that the author died more than 70 years ago, then nothing done in relation to that work will infringe copyright in it. This provision does not apply to Crown copyright works and works vested in international organisations.

6 Recordings of folksongs   A sound recording of a performance of a song can be made for inclusion in an archive maintained by a designated body without infringing copyright in the words of the song or the musical work, provided that the words are unpublished and of unknown authorship and the making of the recording is not prohibited by the performer.

7 Artistic works on public display   UK law allows the photography or the making of a graphic work representing a building, or a sculpture or work of artistic craftsmanship which is permanently situated in a public place or in premises open to the public. This is of some possible use to museums in that they can currently argue that a sculpture in their collection which

is permanently publicly accessible may be photographed by them although of course it also means that members of the public may photograph the sculpture as well.

8   Playing of sound recordings by charities   Playing a sound recording as part of the activities of a 'club, society or other organisation' will not infringe copyright in the sound recording, provided that (i) the organisation is not established or conducted for profit and its main objects are charitable or otherwise concerned with the advancement of education, and (ii) the proceeds of any charge for admission are applied solely for the purposes of the organisation. This may well apply to museums (although there are no decisions on the point) but a licence to perform the music may still be required.

These general provisions aside, there are in the UK no provisions specifically applying to museums. The criticism and review provisions would not extend to reproduction by a museum of images of in-copyright works in its collections for the purposes of conservation or of fulfilling its duty of educating the public. A museum wishing to exploit images of objects in its collection, or copies of such objects – whether commercially or not – must therefore in most cases either make sure that it owns the relevant copyrights, or get the permission of the copyright holders. There is no exception to this rule. Copyright offers no option on public access without control of the copyright.

Museums and galleries are therefore in a difficult position. They are legally obliged under their founding charters to consider the public benefit of their activities. For example, the Boards of Trustees of the Victoria and Albert Museum and the Science Museum are expressly enjoined by statute '*generally (to) promote the public's enjoyment and understanding*' of, respectively, art, craft and design, and science and technology. The National Gallery, Tate Gallery, National Portrait Gallery and Wallace Collection have similar duties. Most other museums have similar objectives.

Fulfilling these objectives surely involves the reproduction and publication (whether in digital or analogue form) of images of objects in the museum or gallery collections. The creation of reproductions in the form of digital images and their publication, for example via the Internet, will involve an infringement of any copyright in those objects. As we have seen, many such objects may well still be in copyright. However, there is little in current UK copyright law which allows museums and galleries to fulfil these objectives without infringing any such copyright.

Museums are therefore on the horns of a dilemma. They are under a duty to disseminate information about their collections as widely as possible; yet UK copyright law currently recognises no public benefit gateway to enable them to achieve this objective without substantial investment in copyright fees and royalties. This seems an unjust position on policy grounds in a situation where, for example, UK law currently allows commercial sale rooms, galleries and auction houses to copy an artistic work for the purpose of advertising the sale of the work.

2.6 EXPLOITATION OF COPYRIGHT

Exploitation generally

As we have seen, owners of copyright in artistic and literary works have considerable control over the use and development of these works. Some museums and galleries are in the fortunate position of having ownership of copyright in parts of their collection. This may be as a result of bequests, or of purchase of the copyright at the same time as acquisition of the work, or perhaps as the result of the museums' or galleries' own extra photographic or design efforts in respect of the original copyright works. This section considers the variety of commercial options open to owners of copyright and the methods used to exploit ownership to achieve the maximum potential 'return'.

With most commercial organisations, 'return' invariably means profit, revenue streams and money in the bank. Several of the world's largest and most complex industries, including the sound recording, film, music and book publishing industries use the ownership and licensing of copyright works to generate considerable commercial returns, and the value of copyrights owned by these industries is immense.

In the world of museums and galleries, many of which are run as charitable organisations or generally as non-profit institutions, the issue of 'return' in connection with the exploitation of copyright is not as straightforward.

There is usually a delicate balance to be struck between the traditional aim of the museum or gallery to make its collection as widely available to the public as possible, and the increasing necessity for those same museums and galleries to fund their operations from 'self-generated' resources. With public and private subsidies in ever-increasing decline, and the rise in expectations in relation to education and recreation, it is not surprising that museums and galleries are forced to examine their collections for untapped potential and to create commercial opportunities from the assets of which they are custodians. This requires assessment of the financial viability of projects, the possible necessity of the recruitment of new staff and critical analysis of the appointment of external contractors and the types of 'deals' and terms on offer. It is principally this latter aspect which will be dealt with in this section.

In giving guidance on the type of commercial terms that can be expected and should be sought from contractors, it is nevertheless important to understand that in the world of commerce, very little is in reality completely standard. Much will depend on the relative bargaining power of the respective parties to the agreement. There is, for example, a difference between dealing on a large publisher's 'standard terms' and dealing on terms that are 'standard in the publishing industry'. Particularly in the areas of new media, electronic rights and the Internet, there are no immutable standards.

One of the results of uncertainty and nervousness in copyright industries is a natural tendency to assume that the safest option in all circumstances is to insist on owning all rights pertaining to copyright for the full term of copyright in every country in the world. While this may be sensible advice in strictly legal terms, and while it does assist in keeping licensing deals from becoming too

43

complex, it also has disadvantages. For a start, it is clearly not possible for both parties to an agreement to follow the policy that full rights ownership must be had at any cost. Compromise on this aspect will become an increasingly important area to address. Furthermore, the complete 'stripping' of rights from individuals can be legally impossible to achieve in some jurisdictions (such as France and Germany) where respect for the rights of authors is more pronounced than in 'common law' jurisdictions such as the UK, USA, Australia and Canada. Finally, there is an argument that the tendency to 'stockpile' rights within institutions that do not have the concomitant skills, initiative and commercial imperative to use or develop them, may unnecessarily deprive creative people of much of the 'bedrock' of their portfolios. This may, in the longer term, unwittingly act as a brake on the development of ideas and techniques.

While many in the commercial world do not have the luxury of being able always to have regard to the long-term effects of their commercial arrangements, the museum and gallery sector has perhaps a special sensitivity and awareness of the 'longer term'. It should not necessarily lose this awareness, when dealing with aspects of making money. It is against this background that this section examines some of the more 'common or garden' varieties of commercial opportunities available to the sector.

Licensing

'Licensing', 'Rights', 'Permissions' and 'Assignments' are all terms used in copyright industries to describe common forms of contractual agreements in such industries. Under these agreements, an entity which owns or controls copyright allows another entity to engage in acts which would otherwise constitute copyright infringement. We will see later how important it is to distinguish clearly between copyright licences and assignments (see section 3.2). Aside from this important distinction, there are many and various types of copyright agreements, reflecting the diversity of the subject matter and type of copyrights involved, the traditions of industries, and the increasingly diverse methods of dealing in copyright works.

Many copyright agreements, particularly licences, follow fairly regular formats and most require a common set of questions to be asked and examined. This section looks at the questions that ought to be asked of most generic forms of dealing in copyright. Not all questions will be relevant. The asking of the question in itself is often however worthwhile.

1   What is the precise legal nature of the parties to the agreement?

In the excitement of commercial negotiations, it can often be easy to overlook the importance of asking who or what is entering into the contract. Only legal entities can enter into contracts. Although it may sound obvious, it is not possible for inanimate objects (such as 'journals') to enter into contracts. Broadly speaking, legal entities include individual people, partnerships and corporate entities. The latter usually have 'Ltd.' or 'Plc' after their name, but not always. In jurisdictions outside the UK, other abbreviations indicating corporate status (and limited liability) exist, including the familiar 'Inc.' of the USA and the perhaps less familiar 'Sarl' or 'GmbH' of France and Germany

44

respectively. In the UK, it is possible for companies limited by guarantee (often registered charities) to dispense with use of the 'Ltd.' nomenclature.

Many museums and galleries in the UK are in fact complex legal entities, often because of their age or the fact that they originated as charitable bequests. The result may be that the institution itself or its trustees do not benefit from the limited liability attaching to most corporations. It is therefore common for such institutions to incorporate a specific subsidiary entity with normal, modern corporate status, which will benefit from the usual ability to limit its liability to the extent of its assets. Tax advantages can also be achieved by the use of such a trading subsidiary and very often, those given the task of exploiting copyrights for museums and galleries will do so through such a subsidiary. Care will need to be taken (see section 3.2) that employees whose copyright work it is expected to be owned by such subsidiaries are in fact employed by the subsidiary, and not some other division of the institution. If the subsidiary itself does not own the rights which it is expected to exploit, then internal assignments, agency or licensing agreements will need to be set in place to give it the power to do so.

Divisions and trading names can be confusing aspects of a legal entity, but they are not always the same as the legal entity itself. A legal entity such as a museum may have several divisions, but unless these have been individually and specifically incorporated, they do not constitute a legal entity that is separate from the museum as a whole. Always be clear about the exact legal entity which is able to and which is required to enter into the agreement. For example, do not give the name of a legal entity which, although related, does not actually own copyright particularly if assurances (also known as warranties) are required in the contract to the effect that the entity has full title to the rights.

The same questions should be asked of the other party to the contract. Unless it is clear that a specific individual is entering into an agreement, always ask questions about the nature of the entity with which business is conducted. If a number of individuals are entering into the agreement, ask if they are a partnership and share accounts and profits between themselves. If they do not, they may be no more than an unincorporated association. So far as possible when dealing with copyright, never contract with unincorporated associations without seeking specific legal advice, as rights ownership here will be complex.

Where dealing with a corporation, always ask whether the individual leading the negotiations has authority to do so. Normally, those with authority will bear the title 'director', 'executive' or 'manager'. Not everyone employed by a company will have the ability to enter into binding agreements on its behalf. If the corporation is unknown and no dealings have been had with it before, the use of credit agencies and publicly available information from Companies House concerning the company is recommended to check its relative soundness.

2 What is the copyright work and what may be done with it?

The former is normally not difficult to establish – it may be a work of art, or the text of a book, or some illustrations. It is important however to identify it properly, by title and author and other distinguishing characteristics if the first two are not conclusive. Often, the finer details will go in a schedule to the agreement.

Of more interest are the rights granted to deal in the copyright work. These are generally the type of rights controlled by copyright, such as reproduction and publication (see generally section 2.5) or subsets of these rights, such as the right to reproduce in digital form or to publish in the English language. It is important to be quite specific when identifying these rights.

3   What is the extent of the grant?

Is the grant to be exclusive, sole or non-exclusive? An exclusive licence is a more valuable right than a sole or non-exclusive licence and in the UK gives special legal rights, akin to full ownership of copyright, to the holder of such a grant. An exclusive licence means that only the licensee is able to exercise the rights granted. A sole licence, by contrast, is usually taken to mean a licence where the grantor also retains the right to exercise the rights granted. A non-exclusive licence is the least valuable, and means that the grantor retains the option to grant identical rights to others. A non-exclusive right is often called a 'permission'.

An allied question is whether the grantee is itself able to pass on the rights in the licence to others. This is known as the right to sub-license or sub-contract. It will be important to have this right if the licensee is essentially in the business of 'organising the project' but may not actually carry out all the steps involved in bringing a copyright product to market. If, for example, a licence is taken to 'reproduce, manufacture and distribute' a copyright work, the licensee will often need the right to sub-license. This will be so if the licensee will not itself be carrying out the process of manufacture, but will be sub-contracting that process to another company, such as a printer or toy manufacturer. As few museums and galleries also double as manufacturers, this is an area in which to exercise care.

4   What territories are to be covered by the grant?

Careful consideration should be given to territorial coverage. For museums and galleries in the UK it is rare to state anything less than the entirety of the United Kingdom. Occasionally, Scotland and Northern Ireland may be segregated if these are regarded as separate markets, subject to the comments below regarding the European Economic Area. The technical definition of the United Kingdom does not include the Channel Islands, the Isle of Man or, of course, the Republic of Ireland so if these are potential markets, they should be specifically stated. Within the European Economic Area (that is, the countries in the European Union plus Norway, Iceland and Liechtenstein) it is not possible for licensees to have complete territorial protection from other countries within the Area particularly where sale and distribution of products is concerned; 'grey' or 'parallel' imports from such countries will always be permissible.

5   What percentage should the royalty be?

'Standard' royalties vary considerably depending on the type of licence under discussion. Books differ from music which differs from branded or specially designed merchandise, and indeed, different types of books differ from each other. Of perhaps more interest, and the area where things often become hazy is the question 'On what amount is the percentage calculated?' What sum of money in the hands of the licensee is subject to the royalty? In most cases, the calculation of this amount will occur in a number of important 'definitions'

46

in the agreement. Often, there will be a definition of something akin to 'Net Receipts' which will cover most forms of income received by the licensee in respect of the exploitation of the copyright work, less an agreed number and type of deductions. The extent of deductions can vary from the standard 'excluding VAT and returns' to the very complex calculations found in film production agreements. Simple formulas are usually the best policy; if there is the possibility of confusion then sample calculations can be set out in a schedule to assist interpretation later when the parties who negotiated and implemented the agreement may have left the businesses concerned. A provision allowing the licensor to check the licensee's accounting methods and calculations is often included and referred to as an 'audit' provision.

6 *What will be the agreed term of the Licence?*

From the perspective of a licensee, a long licence is generally more valuable than a short one. Care should be taken when granting licences in excess of five years as not only do they tie the hands of both parties for a considerable period, but they occasionally raise issues of anti-competitive behaviour.

As important as the agreed term will be the sorts of things that the parties agree will allow them to terminate the agreement early. Most commonly, agreements should provide for early termination if the other party does not comply with important terms of the agreement or if the other party becomes insolvent (in the case of a corporation) or bankrupt (in the case of an individual). It is possible to provide for specific types of behaviour which would be regarded as serious enough to bring the agreement to an end. An example might be a licensee not meeting agreed minimum royalty levels in a specific period or a licensee failing to put appropriate copyright markings on a product. Change of control of either party may also give the parties cause to require termination if, for example, a 'competitor' acquires a licensee.

Sometimes parties use 'initial terms' within which to get to know each other and test the strength and desirability of the commercial relationship. The 'initial term' can be a comparatively short period and the parties may give themselves the unilateral option to cancel the contract at the end of the initial term, before the longer term commences. Ultimately, much will depend on the level of investment and commitment that the parties make to each other in the first instance. If the investment by the licensee is relatively high, it will be more reluctant to agree to an early, one-sided right to cancel by the licensor.

7 *What is the level of commitment and how is it measured?*

It is dangerous to give lengthy, exclusive licences without having some form of guaranteed return from a licensee. At the very least, the licensee should promise to take steps to exploit the copyright work and not merely 'hoard' the rights. At best, a licensor should seek both an advance and a form of minimum royalty or number of sales on which to calculate a royalty to ensure that the licensee has some incentive to do a good job. Sometimes a licensee will take rights to exploit works in developing markets, such as new software platforms, and because of the uncertainty in the market, may be reluctant to accept high levels of commitment. If this is the case, it is often sensible to provide for a 'reversion' of the rights back to the licensor after an agreed period, or for rights to become non-exclusive.

8   Quality control

Any licence which involves the granting of rights in a trade mark or brand should have provisions enabling the museum to check that the mark is being applied to goods which are 'worthy of the brand'. A brand or registered trade mark can quickly lose its value if it is applied to sub-standard merchandise (see section 3.5).

9   'Boilerplate' clauses

Most licensing agreements that have been drawn up by lawyers have a number of fairly general terms that normally appear towards the end of the document. Lawyers refer to these as 'boilerplate', as an indication of their basic and durable nature. Often these terms will include such things as the country of the law governing the agreement, clauses dealing with waiver, clauses preventing any accidental partnership arising between the parties and clauses dealing with events which might unavoidably create problems for the parties, such as the outbreak of war, strikes or natural disasters. It is always worth checking these clauses to ensure that they do accurately reflect the wishes of the parties as even these types of clauses can and do vary considerably in their intent and effect.

Publishing contracts

This is an area which may be familiar to some museum and gallery professionals, particularly those associated with large national or well-known collections. Book publication is still the most common way of promoting a collection and educating the public in connection with it. Even small collections will usually have a catalogue or guide relating to the collection, while large national galleries and museums will have curatorial staff to assist with and create published works. Some even have their own small publishing houses.

From a legal perspective, most book publishing agreements are simply a subset of the general form of licence discussed in section 2.6: Licensing. Most of the same considerations will apply, along with others which are more specific to the type of work and relationship constructed by the licence. There are several good books on publishing agreements, such as Clark, Owen and Palmer's book, *Publishing Agreements*. This work is not intended to replace them.

The most common forms of agreement found in book publishing are:

Author agreements   These commonly take the form of an exclusive licence from the author to the publisher for a fixed period of time (usually a long one, i.e. in excess of 10 years) or for the term of copyright. Exceptions to the principle of granting a licence are compilation works, where the publisher may need to take a full assignment of rights from all contributors in order to ensure that one recalcitrant author is not in a position to prevent full exploitation of the work. Where assignments or very extensive rights are given by the author, the author may expect a 'reversion of rights' at some stage if it becomes clear that the publisher is failing to exploit the work. This may happen if the work has been out of print for an agreed period.

These agreements commonly distinguish between primary rights (the right to publish the book in agreed formats, territories and languages) and so-called 'subsidiary rights'. The latter are rights, the exercise of which requires the permission of the copyright owner (the author), but which the parties agree are best 'administered' by the publisher. The publisher however *only acts as agent* for the author, rather than as licensee. The difference is a considerable one. It is similar to the difference between being the tenant of a house (a licence) and being the estate agent involved in the potential sale of the house (agency agreement). The reason for giving publishers these 'agency' rights is because third parties who are interested in exploiting such rights fully (i.e. by becoming licensees) may tend to approach the publisher in the first instance rather than the author. Major subsidiary rights include film and television rights and translation rights. Of course, the publisher, like any agent, will take a percentage share of any payment secured for the author in respect of a grant of such rights. Authors may also prefer to have their 'subsidiary rights' handled by a professional literary agent instead of their publisher.

In the United Kingdom, the Publishers' Association, the Writers' Guild and the Society of Authors have various guides to general or 'minimum terms agreements' that can usefully be consulted.

Licence of language rights Publishers and authors whose first language is English have a surprisingly large market for the licensing of rights to produce the book in another language to foreign publishers. Usually the licence of the right is in return for a relatively substantial advance, and then a provision for a percentage royalty on sales. In the publishing world, advances are almost always recoupable; that is, they are genuinely 'in advance of and on account of' expected royalties so that no royalty payments will be received until the language publisher has 'recouped' the amount of the advance. Sometimes there is agreement on a specific print run for the publication in which case the sale may simply be for a lump sum. The resultant book will be published under the imprint of the rights' licensee.

Co-edition agreements These are a form of 'mini' joint venture between publishers in which the 'originating' publisher comes up with a proposal for a book which it will need other publishers (usually foreign language publishers) to help fund. This will often be the case for colour books, where the origination and production costs are high. The originating publisher arranges for the production and delivery of the finished works to its partners. A price for the finished version will be agreed. The main issue here is whether the price includes or excludes a number of costs (apart from production), which would normally be associated with the cost of the book. Extra costs to be considered include author royalties, packaging and shipping costs. Again, the resultant book will be sold under the various imprints of the co-edition partners.

3. Current issues and practical solutions

Intel Pentium Microprocessor, USA, 1992 © Science Museum/Science & Society Picture Library

The photograph is protected by copyright. The surface of the microprocessor may well be protected, either by copyright (if the chip was designed before 7 November 1987), by semiconductor topography right (if the topography was created between 7 November 1987 and 31 July 1989) or by design right (if created after 1 August 1989).

3.1 LOSING YOUR ASSETS: ACCESS TO THE COLLECTION

Most museums want as many visitors as possible. Even without admission charges, attendance figures for museums are key: for raising the museum's public profile; for making a case for further local authority or central government support; for increasing sales at the museum shop. But, of course, the main reason for encouraging access is that this is the museum's mission: to reach out and communicate to the public.

The constitutions of all museums that have charitable status and the mission statements of most that do not insist on the advancement of education of the public – and in most cases, this means that the public must come through the door.

But unlimited access to all parts of the collections cannot seriously be contemplated: works may be fragile or light/humidity sensitive and therefore cannot, properly, be on open display; items may be in disrepair or in need of conservation and therefore not appropriate for display; works might be duplicates of lesser quality than better examples in the same museum's collection – or, quite simply, staffing requirements and the size of the gallery might mean that only a small part of the collection can realistically be available for view at any one time.

Before an item can be offered up for public display, a museum will typically invest a great deal of time (and money) over some years. The item must first be acquired; it may well need to be properly identified, researched and curated; conservation or restoration might need to be carried out; display cases, special lighting and humidity controls may need to be commissioned, paid for and installed. Finally, there is cataloguing and publicity before the doors are thrown open, as it were, to the public.

In order for these processes to be carried out, cash is needed. There is acknowledged general opposition to admission charges (and the introduction of these in smaller museums can result in a catastrophic reduction in public access). And local authorities and universities may be loathe to support further the capital and revenue costs of a museum when there may be more pressing immediate needs of more apparent public benefit. But, embarrassingly (and sometimes negligently) perhaps the museum's most likely source of income, its most valuable asset, the intellectual property that it can create, often simply walks out of the door.

In reviewing the term of protection given by current copyright laws, it is apparent that copyright will have expired in the collections of a large number of museums. Even if the museum has more contemporary collections where there may continue to subsist some copyright protection, it is rare for this to be owned by the museum.

In order for museums to raise income from merchandising, licensing or the commercial 'development' of any part of their collections, the museum must quite simply build, somehow, exclusive rights to its collections. This means ensuring that others who might have access to the museum do not take away similar rights when the gates are locked at the end of the day. The two areas that the museum must look to establish are copyright and publication right.

52

The museum, for instance, can begin to build up its own portfolio of copyright material if, in an appropriate and lawful way, it:

- photographs works of art and other items in its collections
- creates souvenirs, or three-dimensional objects, based on sculptures or other material
- copies or adapts old designs, wallpaper patterns, fabric designs
- reprints and restores damaged photographs

Provided the museum uses its own in-house photographers (who carry out the work pursuant to their employment) or it commissions outside photographers on appropriate terms, the photographs and other material created may well be protected by a fresh copyright which would not expire until at least 70 years after the end of the year in which the photographer or maker died – and these copyrights to be owned by the museum. The museum can then, in turn, merchandise these images itself (or license them to others in return for a royalty). However, there is a potential problem. Copyright law does not grant a monopoly; it does not claim that only one copyright image can exist at any one time of a particular object.

Example: There are tens of thousands of tourists who, each year, take photographs of Buckingham Palace. They may not be doing anything particularly novel; their photographs may look almost identical – but they will each have an independent copyright which they will own in each frame of each film that they take. The descendants of the owner of the first photograph taken of the Palace cannot prevent others from taking similar pictures.

There is no reason why such images even of public domain objects cannot be licensed – the real problem is not the copyright laws but the fact that there are many competing originals. And if there is more than one original why should anyone single out any one particular copyright owner?

There can therefore be more than one picture of 'the changing of the guard' on offer at any one time worldwide. Each picture will have its own copyright. The same applies to museum collections. Any other person who has (or has had) any access to the museum collection whether in its galleries or in store and has taken photographs can, unless they have contracted otherwise, use that material for their own personal purposes. They can also sell the photographs, assign copyright or license publishers. The fact that the trustees own the physical pieces is simply not relevant.

If the museum then goes out into the market place offering 'exclusive pictures' then it may well have lost the game already. Other competing material will already be out there and potential merchandising arms (such as Corbis or the Bridgeman Art Library) will be more reluctant or unwilling to take on the material and open up the income stream for the museum.

What can the museum do? The museum must secure the exclusivity; it must require that no person who has access to its collections either on site, or taken away for research purposes, or loaned elsewhere, can be permitted to take photographs, recordings, copies or other reproductions except on specific terms agreed in advance with the museum.

53

How is this exclusivity obtained? Three basic forms are needed:

- an agreement with freelance photographers
- a form of permission for photography within the gallery
- location filming agreement

These are all set out in the sample agreements (Appendix 4.3).

Agreement with freelance photographers

It is widely believed that if one commissions an outside designer or photographer and pays that person then, on delivery of the originals, the museum automatically becomes the owner of all rights. This is false. Current copyright law insists that, subject to a few minor exceptions, it is the creator of the original work (the photographer or designer) who will be the first owner of the copyright in that material – even if the work has been commissioned – and even if he or she has been paid (in full) by another.

Where creative work has been commissioned, the museum will naturally have some sort of agreed usage (known as a licence) for the material – but it will not be the copyright owner. Invariably, the photographer, illustrator, writer or designer will still have residual rights for the exploitation of that material. They could place the material with an agency or picture library, license it themselves or indeed sell on the copyright.

In the Appendices, there is a specimen agreement and brief for commissioned photography. This covers:

- the basic terms on which a photographer may have access to the galleries, but critically that
- the photographer assigns, outright to the museum, the copyright in the photographs when taken.

Permission for photography in the gallery

For a few hundred pounds, any amateur can purchase a high quality camera with auto-focus and automatic exposure and can take, with a little care and without the need for special lighting or tripods, high quality photographs suitable for professional reproduction. Coupled with new generation films which operate in a wide range of lighting conditions and can be pushed from 100 to 1000 ASA, it should be plain that any casual visitor with a camera can produce a set of photographs suitable for reproduction and licensing. In other words, such a visitor could, for all practical purposes, acquire their own set of photographs and then compete with any photographs which the museum might be hoping to commercialise.

It is, in practice, impossible to discriminate between a snap-happy tourist and a scheming intruder who has half an eye on producing professional quality material for licensing elsewhere. Accordingly, if the museum does want to retain exclusive rights to the photographs it has taken or commissioned of the pictures or items on display then it must ensure that it, alone, has such photographs. No photography can therefore be allowed in the gallery save where specific permission has been given.

A museum is really confronted with two options:

1 a decision to ban all photography within the galleries outright save where there is a specific written request for the photography of one or two named works of art or objects and the terms for any permission given negotiated in advance, or

2 a looser approach where the museum concedes that it really can have no monopoly

Curators, those involved in merchandising and the museum director must all discuss and agree policy with regard to

● whether photography is allowed in the gallery/museum

● whether the use of tripod and flash are permitted

● whether, if photography is permitted, it must be subject to signing a photographic permission form

● whether there are any key items in the collections which are so central to the museum's merchandising activities that no photography can be allowed

● what photography can be allowed if any, within the archives

● the access that researchers, students and other persons may have to the collections

● the possibility of their photographing such items and how, and to what extent, this might affect potential merchandising

● importantly, the conditions under which any work may be removed from the museum or gallery for any purpose whether for restoration, research, loan or scholarship

Consideration must also be given to any form of filming within the museum or gallery, press releases and sending out images; and more generally, access to old out of copyright material which has never been communicated to the public. Although there may not be a copyright problem, the matter must be taken into account following a thorough consideration of the potential of publication right (see section 3.4).

3.2 LOOSE CANNONS – CURATORS, CONSULTANTS AND COMMISSIONS

Employees

As we have seen (see section 2.4), the copyright in works created by an employee in the course of his/her employment belongs to his/her employer, subject to any agreement to the contrary.

This suggests that, by and large, museums can assume that they own the copyright in works created by museum staff in the course of their duties, and that these copyrights can then be exploited for the benefit of the museum. Examples of such works would be text for exhibition panels written by curators and photographs taken by photographers on the museum's staff (see section 2.4 on the question of who is or is not to be regarded as an 'employee'). In the same way, the copyright in catalogues of objects in the museum's collections will, where they have been written by curators on the museum's staff, belong to the museum.

However, this assumption may not always hold true. The above examples are instances of works which are clearly related to the museum's core activities – the exhibition, curation and conservation of the museum's collections. Curators, as distinct perhaps from other staff employed by museums such as administrative staff, or indeed staff employed by a museum's trading company, may well be engaged in other academic pursuits. These may well be an accepted part of the curator's activities. The curator may be invited to give lectures about their area of specialisation, or to write books about it. The curator may take their own photographs of objects in the museum's collection. The question then arises of who owns the copyright in these works.

In some cases, it may be clear that the works were not created as part of the curator's duties. For example, the curator may have been commissioned to write a book by a publisher and have written the book entirely in their spare time, without using any of the museum's equipment. The copyright in the book would belong to the curator (although there might be a question arising under the employment contract if it contained a term prohibiting staff from writing works that competed with the museum's own publications). It is of course going to be difficult in some cases to say whether any such work was created by the curator in their spare time or not. However, the terms of the employment contract (and in particular the job description) ought to contain a clear guide on what the curator is employed to do.

In other cases there may, as in the academic community at large (though not by any means consistently), be a 'contrary agreement' whereby the curator retains copyright in certain works. It may be accepted practice for curators to use their time while in the employment of museums to write lectures, articles and books which the curators can then exploit on their own, without any suggestion that the museum owns copyright in the text.

It may not be comfortable for museums to confront the issue of copyright in curators' works. Equally, any suggestion that anything written or created by curators while employed by the museum might belong to the museum may not be palatable to curators. However, museums are looking increasingly to assets such as copyright to help generate the revenue streams necessary to support their core activities, and indeed to enable them to continue to employ curators. It must therefore be in the interests both of museums and curators to work out an appropriate *modus vivendi* to maximise and share the possible return from curators' expertise.

Commissioning

If the copyright in works created by an employee in the course of employment generally belongs to the employer, the corollary is that copyright in works created by persons not employed by the museum, such as freelances and independent contractors, remains with those persons unless assigned to the museum (see section 2.4).

It is therefore vital for any museum wishing to obtain maximum freedom of action in relation to commissioned works to obtain an assignment of copyright or at the very least a licence allowing the museum to make adequate use of the works in question.

There are countless examples of copyright works which are commissioned by museums. Some very few museums are in the fortunate position of commissioning works to add to their collections. But those that are not will need to commission third parties to do work that cannot always be done by museum staff, for example designing a new gallery or gallery installations, photographing objects in the collections, writing software for interactive exhibits. In any of these cases, the museum ought to try to secure an assignment or licence of copyright to allow the museum to reproduce the work in question.

This pre-supposes a consistent museum policy and, ideally, a set of standard commissioning terms that make clear that, in return for payment, the copyright will be assigned. The importance of this cannot be over-emphasised in relation to photographs and indeed films of objects in the museum's own collections (see section 3.1).

It is equally important for curators to understand the significance of securing copyright assignments. There is a perception in some quarters that securing copyright is unimportant when set against the museum's overriding duty to disseminate information about its collections to the public. There is no question that museums have such a duty. However, securing copyright can help museums achieve a number of objectives:

1   it enables museums to secure an asset that can (even if only in a modest way) help to generate funds to support the museum's activities and fulfil its educative objectives;

2   it ensures that museums do not have to pay another copyright holder each time they wish to reproduce the work or image;

3   it transfers the discretion as to how the copyright should be exploited to the museum, and out of the hands of others who may have no public interest agenda to serve.

Assignment or licence?

The preceding paragraphs leave open the possibility of securing the copyright by means of an assignment or a licence. The difference between these two transactions is dealt with in section 2.4. The advantage of an assignment is clearly that ownership, and therefore complete control, of the copyright is obtained. However, where the museum is dealing with a commercially aware party then an assignment may be difficult to obtain at a sensible price.

Since copyright is a bundle of rights, each of which can be extracted and dealt with separately, it may be more commercially viable to acquire a licence to do those things with the copyright work which the museum needs to do. It may be the case that the work in question is not available except under a non-exclusive licence. For example, a licence to use a photograph from a picture library is very likely only to be available on non-exclusive terms.

However, where a work has been specifically commissioned by a museum, for example for a particular gallery (e.g. gallery designs) or text for a catalogue, then careful thought should be given to whether an assignment or a licence should be obtained. Such works are often intended to be uniquely connected with the museum. They may well have been commissioned on the understanding that they will not be reproduced elsewhere. In these circumstances, an assignment would not be inappropriate or unreasonable. The same would certainly be true of works acquired as part of the museum's collections (as to which, see section 3.3).

So far as museum publications are concerned, the commercial imperative would suggest that generally, it would be in the museum's interest to acquire the copyright in works commissioned or prepared for such publications by way of an assignment. The museum would then be in a position to exploit these works freely and in any medium without having to re-negotiate terms with the author each time. This is not always possible, and the extent of the rights which the museum can acquire will be a matter of negotiation, depending on the circumstances. However, where an assignment cannot be obtained, an exclusive licence is the next best thing. Certainly, so far as any works which the museum intends to exploit commercially are concerned, an exclusive licence should be sought.

Whatever the basis on which it is appropriate to proceed, the museum must assess its requirements at the outset and make clear at the *beginning* of any negotiation with authors, photographers, artists and other creators that these are the conditions on which the museum is prepared to commission the work. This may seem an unattractively commercial approach for a museum to take. There are two answers to this:

1 copyright is an economic right and hence a commercial asset;

2 it is the duty of the museum, as a charity, to maximise its opportunities for exploiting its assets in the fulfilment of its charitable (i.e. educational) objectives.

If a museum does not negotiate appropriate terms, it may find itself obstructed in the fulfilment of those very objectives, because a third party will be able to determine whether the copyright work in question may be reproduced or not.

Assignment/licence to the museum or its trading company?

As has been made clear, copyright is an economic right which can be exploited commercially. This commercial exploitation poses problems for museums, the vast majority of which are charities (in the case of the national museums, exempt charities). Licensing copyright is a trade, which could potentially prejudice a museum's charitable status unless the licensing activity is conducted in pursuit of the museum's primary purposes (e.g. educating the public).

However some forms of publishing may not be in fulfilment of the museum's primary purposes (e.g. licensing images for reproduction on merchandise). The way in which charities can benefit from trading activity without prejudicing their charitable status is to establish a wholly-owned trading subsidiary which covenants its profits to the charity. This is as true of museums as of any other charities.

The question therefore arises of whether any copyrights should be assigned or licensed to the museum or to its trading subsidiary. If a museum carries on any trading which is not in furtherance of its charitable objectives, then the receipts generated by such trading will, strictly, be assessable to tax (unless the proportion of such receipts falls below certain limits). One of the virtues of a trading subsidiary is that it can conduct trading which is not in furtherance of the museum's charitable objectives, without prejudicing the museum's right to recover tax on the profits covenanted up from the company.

Certainly some of the trading carried out with copyrights may be in furtherance of a museum's charitable objectives. However, some trading may not and, by and large, licensing intellectual property such as copyright and trade marks for a royalty is treated by the Revenue as trading which should be subject to a tax charge.

The trustees of a museum are under a positive duty to make the best of the charity's assets for the benefit of the charity, which includes mitigating any tax liability. However, assigning a copyright to a trading subsidiary does mean that the asset is vulnerable to the insolvency of the trading subsidiary. This should be a hypothetical concern given that the purpose of the trading subsidiary is to be run for profit.

There are various possible solutions. Unfortunately, none of them have yet been the subject of specific Revenue approval. In these circumstances, it may be judged safest to put copyrights which are commercially exploited into the trading subsidiary or (to avoid the risk of insolvency) a special purpose vehicle controlled by the trustees which can then license the trading subsidiary.

Warranties and indemnities

Whether the copyright in a work is assigned or licensed to the museum, the museum needs to consider protecting that investment by seeking appropriate warranties, possibly backed up by an indemnity.

Warranties are effectively promises that the copyright has not been dealt with in a way which would reduce its value in the hands of the museum. The person assigning or licensing copyright would warrant, for example, that they are indeed the owner of the copyright and have not granted any rights to a third party that would conflict with those being granted to the museum. Further examples of such warranties appear in the sample agreements in Appendix 4.3.

It is normal for such warranties to be accompanied by an indemnity. This is essentially a contractual undertaking to compensate a purchaser of copyright rights fully for any losses and expenses suffered or incurred as a result of the assignor's/licensor's breach of warranty – for example where it turns out that the assignor/licensor had granted the rights twice over, with the result that the museum is infringing the rights of the first assignee/licensee. Again, examples of indemnities appear in the sample agreements in Appendix 4.3.

3.3 BUILDING THE FOUNDATIONS – ACQUISITIONS AND EXHIBITIONS

Why copyright should be considered at the outset

The first opportunity for a museum to assess the copyright status of an object is on acquisition. Information about copyright ownership can become harder to obtain over time (memories fade, documents get lost). It is much more expensive to trace the copyright owner when an object has been in the collection for years than to address the question of copyright ownership at the outset.

From an administrative point of view it should be relatively straightforward for a museum to require that the copyright owner be identified, and the museum's rights to reproduce the object established, on acquisition. Each object has to undergo a proper curatorial assessment prior to acquisition. When the relevant details of the object are added to the collections management database, copyright should (where relevant) be dealt with at the same time. Checking the museum's rights to reproduce any object which is a copyright work should therefore be part of this whole process.

Another good reason for dealing with copyright in an object when it is acquired is that it can (though not always) be easier to negotiate an assignment of the copyright, or a licence on more generous terms than would be possible later. Once the museum has acquired the object, its bargaining position is weakened by its wish to reproduce it for some specific purpose such as a publication or an exhibition. The value of the copyright is then obvious, making it easier for the holder of the copyright to seek some consideration in return (e.g. a sizeable licence fee). It is also often the case that, by the time the museum wishes to reproduce the work, the copyright is no longer owned or controlled by the creator of the work (e.g. the artist) but by the artist's estate, or by a commercial entity that has bought the rights (e.g. a publishing house), or by an agency representing the artist's estate (e.g. DACS). In each case the person(s) owning or controlling the copyright will naturally be concerned to ensure that any transaction involving copyright exploitation by the museum generates value, whether in the form of licence fees, royalties or otherwise. In the case of DACS there is a positive duty to generate royalty income.

By contrast, the situation when a work is acquired tends to be more favourable to the museum. The donor may also be the owner of the copyright (this would obviously be the case where the museum is being given the work by its creator). Experience shows that it can be much easier to deal with the copyright question at this stage. Artists are often only too happy to give the museum the benefit of the copyright at the same time as the work is acquired. It is not unheard of for an artist's estate to be more jealous in guarding the copyright than the artist.

Of course, the ease of obtaining the copyright on acquisition should not be exaggerated. The situation will be different where a museum is purchasing the work rather than receiving a donation. Nevertheless, the atmosphere is far more conducive to securing the copyright rights which a museum needs when a work is acquired than when the museum needs a licence to reproduce a work already in its possession.

Who owns the copyright?

As we have emphasised many times already (see section 2.1), the person who owns the work itself may *not* necessarily be the person who owns the copyright in it. If the museum is considering the question of copyright on an acquisition, it is vital for it to appreciate this fact.

It can happen that the owner of the work and the owner of the copyright are one and the same person – for example the artist or writer, or an heir who has inherited both the work and the copyright. But in many cases ownership is split. The copyright might have been assigned by the artist during his/her lifetime to someone else.

Alternatively, a share of the copyright may remain with the owner of the copyright work, but another share may belong to someone else. For example, in the case of a film, the copyright may be divided between the producer and the director. There may be more than one owner of the same copyright (see section 2.4).

In only one case is ownership of the copyright presumed to pass with ownership of the object. This is where an original document or other material thing embodying an *unpublished* literary, dramatic or artistic work is bequeathed by will. Unless there is a contrary intention expressed in the testator's will (or a codicil), the copyright is presumed to pass with the object provided, of course, that the testator owned the copyright immediately before their death.

Tracing the copyright owner

Anyone experienced in dealing with copyright will say that finding the copyright owner can be one of the most time-consuming and frustrating of tasks. Yet it is certainly worth doing if the ultimate objective is to acquire an asset of value such as copyright.

The UK system of copyright does not depend on registration of title. There is therefore no register in the UK which can be inspected to reveal who owns the copyright in any given object. Instead, copyright ownership has to be traced laboriously by identifying the creator of the work, and then working from there to check the employment status of the creator at the time he/she created the work (see section 2.4), whether the creator left a will and, if so, what it said and so on.

In the USA there are still advantages in registering a work for copyright at the US Copyright Office, so there can be some advantage in checking to see whether the US Copyright Office's records reveal anything, especially in the case of works that are or were exploited in the USA.

If the copyright owner cannot be traced by reasonable enquiry then clearly the museum cannot acquire the copyright, but there may be other steps it can take (see section 2.5: Anonymous works).

Donations

Whenever a museum is being offered the gift of an object for its collections which may either be in copyright or is an unpublished work, it should consider the copyright status of the object and, if possible, take an assignment of the copyright at the same time as the donation. If a full assignment is not possible a licence to reproduce the object for the museum's purposes should be sought at the very least. The museum should ensure that all who are responsible for managing acquisitions should be aware of any copyright policy adopted by the museum, and that they are equipped with suitable documentation.

Bequests

Museums often receive bequests of objects by will. Sometimes it is too late to do anything about securing that the copyright is also bequeathed in the will (assuming that the testator is the copyright owner). In that case the museum will need to approach the executors of the will to find out who may be the beneficiary of the copyright, and then try to acquire the copyright from that beneficiary. It may be that the will is silent on the subject of copyright, in which case, if the work is unpublished, the museum can claim the copyright itself (see section 2.4: Unpublished works bequeathed by will).

However, especially in the case of major bequests, there may well be an opportunity to discuss the terms of the bequest before the testator's death. This may be the case, for example, where works are bequeathed and accepted in lieu of inheritance tax. Alternatively, a series of works may be bequeathed all at once. It would certainly be worthwhile for a museum in this fortunate position to check the copyright position.

Moral rights can be disposed of by will (although they may not be assigned). Indeed, the owner of moral rights is, under UK law, free to leave the moral rights to anyone by will. If the museum is in any position to influence the terms of a bequest, then it ought to consider including a disposition that the moral rights pass to the museum as well as the copyright – provided that the museum is content to become the custodian of these rights. The museum would not be under any obligation to exercise them, but it may well regard the ability to require the artist to be properly identified, or to object to derogatory treatment of a work, as useful (see section 3.4).

Purchases

The question of copyright should be as relevant to any purchase of an object as it is to a donation or a bequest. However, a purchase usually involves a negotiation on price. If the seller is also the copyright owner, then requiring an assignment of copyright may naturally have an effect on the price. That said, it is arguably easier to negotiate a reasonable premium to include the copyright on a purchase of the work than on a subsequent separate negotiation involving the copyright alone.

If the seller of the work does not own the copyright in it then the copyright owner will need to be traced (see section 3.3: Tracing the copyright owner, above).

The museum should certainly consider the usual warranties and indemnities on a purchase of the copyright (see section 3.2). It may be harder to negotiate warranties and indemnities where the work is being donated.

Lending and borrowing

One of the reasons why it is worth acquiring the copyright in a work at the outset is that the museum is then in a position to grant suitable licences to other museums and galleries when the work is loaned for an exhibition.

It is, of course, simpler for the lending museum to require of the borrowing institution that it obtain all clearances from the copyright owner enabling the borrowing institution to reproduce the work in connection with its exhibition. However, since the copyright owner may not give clearance, or not without charging a large fee, the lending museum will be fulfilling its duty to advance the understanding and enjoyment of the work by the public if it has secured control of the copyright and can grant a licence to the borrowing institution.

If, however, the lending museum does not own the copyright in the object itself, the usual arrangement is for the borrowing institution to obtain the necessary copyright clearances at its own cost, as part of the terms of the loan. Such a provision needs to appear in the loan agreement.

Quite separately from the copyright (if any) in the object itself, copyright will subsist in any photographs of the object which are made available by the lending museum. Copyright in such photographs ought to belong to the lending museum, provided that the proper procedures have been followed (see section 3.1). The loan agreement, or a separate document negotiated in parallel, needs to provide for copyright in the photographs and in particular to deal with the following matters:

1 what rights are being granted to the borrowing institution and whether these last for only as long as the exhibition (plus a reasonable sell-off period) or for longer;

2 what warranties are offered by the lending museum in respect of the copyright in the photographs;

3 the quality of reproduction;

4 the safe-keeping of the transparencies, and when they should be returned.

As explained above, the rental or lending of the original or copies of a copyright work to the public infringes the copyright unless licensed (see section 2.5). However, the expressions 'rental' and 'lending' do *not* include making available for the purpose of public exhibition or making the original work or copies (e.g. photographs or prints) available between establishments that are accessible to the public. Loans *between* museums and galleries should therefore never infringe rental or lending rights in a copyright work, whether for the purposes of public exhibition or for scholarly or research purposes.

Where the museum is the borrowing institution, however, the lender may not be another museum or 'establishment accessible to the public'. If the loan is for the purposes of public exhibition, the rental or lending right should not be infringed. However, if a private lender is lending a work to a museum for purposes *other* than public exhibition, the borrowing museum may be able to rely on the exception permitting 'on-the-spot reference use'. If not, a licence may need to be obtained from the copyright owner.

As indicated above, it is often the case that the borrowing institution is required to obtain copyright clearances as a term of any loan of a copyright work. From the perspective of a museum borrowing a work for an exhibition, the following matters will need to be considered:

1   whether the work borrowed is in copyright and, if so, who is the copyright owner;

2   what licences need to be obtained from the copyright owner to enable the borrowing museum to exhibit the work in public and reproduce it (e.g. on posters, postcards and in the exhibition catalogue);

3   whether the lender requires the borrower to use only transparencies supplied by the lender and, if so, on what terms, or whether the borrower is free to take its own photographs of the loaned object;

4   if the lender does require the borrower to use only the lender's transparencies, what warranties the lender can offer as to ownership of copyright in the transparencies (as opposed to the copyright, if any, in the loaned object).

If an object is being loaned for a touring exhibition then it would be sensible for the lead institution to co-ordinate any negotiations with copyright owners to ensure that licences are granted on favourable terms to all the museums involved, subject to some reasonable compensation from the other museums to cover the lead institution's administrative costs. Such co-ordination would be particularly desirable where many of the objects concerned are in copyright, or where many rights are involved (for example in the case of audio-visual material).

3.4 LINGERING RIGHTS – ARTISTS AND ARCHIVES

Copyright and other rights

Whether or not copyright subsists in a particular work has already been looked at. We have also seen how the museum itself may obtain copyright protection for a work that it creates.

Quite often, the question 'Who owns the copyright in this work?' does not disclose the complete answer. There may be other rights which linger and which, effectively, can limit the use of the material – even if the museum has the rights from the copyright owner or is, indeed, the copyright owner itself.

Overlapping copyrights

A photograph taken by a curator of, say, an ancient shrunken head is unlikely to cause copyright difficulties. There may be conservation factors and other controls regarding the material itself – but, in relation to the photograph, in most cases, it will be clear: the curator, if he/she has taken the photograph as part of their employment will have passed the copyright over, automatically, to the museum. The museum then has all the rights it needs.

However, if the photograph is of, say, a twentieth-century work of art, then it is likely that, even though the museum will nevertheless own the copyright in the photograph (and the work itself), the photograph typically cannot be reproduced without the consent of the owner of the copyright in that work.

Example: a gallery decides to put on a show of popular culture from the 1950s. It prepares a poster and catalogue cover based on a collage of 150 reduced size images of portraits and photographs of influential 1950s characters as well as photographs of cars, sporting events and some classic advertising shots by famous French photographers. All the images are reproduced complete but reduced to a small size to make a mosaic pattern on the poster and catalogue cover. Here, if no permissions have been obtained the gallery is laying itself open to numerous claims from individual copyright owners. Size of the image is not relevant and only one copyright owner need complain in order to prevent sale of the poster.

Publication right

Once an original work has been identified and it has been ascertained that copyright, if it ever existed, would long since have expired, there is a residual question of publication right. This right can arise where copyright has expired and subsequently the work is then republished or communicated to the public in some form, e.g. by exhibition. Publication right could arise where the museum or gallery has, negligently, or inadvertently, released the material to someone else who has then carried on one of the necessary acts in order for publication right to come into existence.

It is conceivable that there might be more than one original: a sculptor might have cast more than one original artist's proof; an artist might have pulled several trial prints from the same etching plate but never released the prints to the public. Separate originals each the same, could be in separate hands. Even if the gallery has access to one of the originals, the publication right might conceivably have arisen elsewhere. Thought needs to be given in each case, as to whether this possibility could conceivably arise.

Publication right is explored in more detail in 3.4: Publication right, below.

Moral rights

These are rights given to the original creator of a literary, dramatic, musical or artistic work. They allow them to control the way in which that work is used or reproduced – and the control continues even if they no longer physically possess that work and even if they have ceased to be the copyright owner.

Moral rights are so called because they are not economic in nature (they cannot, in general, be bought and sold and the rights cannot be licensed in return for a royalty). They guard, however, the creator's reputation and honour.

These rights have their origins in the 'Droit Moral' system from continental Europe – and derive from a position that authors should, independently of their economic rights, continue to have some relationship with their works. Their works are an expression of their artistry and character, and the authors and artists can, and should be able to, retain some control over the way in which their works are presented to the public.

The rights of the author are as follows:

- the right to be identified as author or director: 'the right of paternity';
- the right not to have their work subjected to 'derogatory treatment': 'the integrity right';
- the right not to have the work falsely attributed to them;
- there is also a privacy right of a person in relation to photographs commissioned for private or domestic purposes.

A brief outline of the rights are as follows:

The right of paternity

Relevant works   Copyright literary, dramatic, musical or artistic works or films.

The person in whose favour the right is granted   The author (or in the case of a film, the director).

The nature of the right   The right to be identified as author or director respectively.

The right is for the author to be identified as the author of the work whenever it is communicated in some form to the public. This covers publication, performance, broadcast of the work, inclusion in films and, in the special case of artistic works, when the work is exhibited in public or when it is installed in public.

Duration of the right   The same as the term of copyright for the relevant work.

Requirement for the right   There is a pre-condition that the right must first be formally asserted. This can be done either generally or specifically. The right can be 'asserted' in three ways:

- In a document assigning copyright (this typically will give notice to anyone who becomes the copyright owner)
- By specific notice (most published books now have the assertion set out in the frontispiece) often in similar form to the following:

'The rights of the author to be identified are asserted in accordance with Copyright, Designs and Patents Act 1988' or

66

'The right of (name of author) to be identified as the author of this work has been asserted in accordance with sections 77 and 78 of the Copyright, Designs and Patents Act 1988'

- By the identification of the author on an original artistic work either on the original or copy, or on the frame or mount or plinth to which it is attached.

Surprisingly, the legislation states that assertion in this last way binds any person into whose hands the original or copy comes whether or not the identification is still present or visible.

Exceptions   There are limited exceptions in respect of:

- all works where the author died prior to 1 August 1989
- computer programs
- typeface designs
- computer generated work
- Crown copyright and parliamentary copyright
- copyright originally vested in certain international organisations
- where the copyright has vested in someone else and any act is done by or with the licence of the copyright owner
- where the artistic work is incidentally included in another work
- where the work is reproduced fairly for the purpose of reporting current events by means of a sound recording, film broadcast and cable programme
- in relation to any work (other than photographs) reproduced for the purposes of reporting current events
- certain limitations in relation to publication in periodicals, encyclopaedias, dictionaries, year books or other collective works

    Comment: *By reason of the first exception set out above, most older works will be excluded from the requirement to comply with the paternity right – but certainly in relation to any text or other literary work, photograph or artistic work created since August 1989 care should be taken to consider the question of a credit before any publication or public exhibition.*

In general, it would be prudent, and indeed good practice to credit any author with their original work particularly in relation to exhibitions, posters, catalogues and promotional material.

The right to object to derogatory treatment

Requirements   Unlike in relation to the right of paternity, there is no requirement that the right should first be 'asserted'.

When is the right available?

The author must show that the work has been:

1 subject to a 'treatment' – in other words any addition to, deletion from or alteration to or adaptation of the work.

   This therefore covers the cropping of any photographs or images, editing of text (however small) or the cutting of any frames from film footage

   and

2 that the treatment has been 'derogatory'.

   This is central to the right. The treatment is derogatory if it amounts to:

   • a distortion of the work,

   • a mutilation of the work, or

   • is otherwise prejudicial to the honour or reputation of the author or director.

It is not clear from the legislation whether the precise words 'prejudicial to the honour or reputation of the author or director' also qualify the words 'distortion' and/or 'mutilation'.

Consideration however of the original Copyright Convention (Berne Convention on the Protection of Artistic and Literary Works) from which the provisions derive indicate that this is the case: prejudice must therefore be shown to the honour or reputation of the author in the way in which the work is treated whether there is distortion, mutilation or other treatment.

> **Comment:** *Great care should be taken in relation to posters for exhibitions, display stands, catalogue covers and other uses or imagery of text. Has there been any editing of the text? Has there been any cropping or digital manipulation of the imagery?*

In one case proceedings were brought by a well-known cartoonist against a national museum for allegedly misusing cartoons which were changed in size and re-coloured. Artists are sensitive to the way in which their work is presented and museums must respect such sensitivities.

Exhibition designers, and the merchandising arms of any museum, must therefore be alert to any reproduction of works which are still in copyright. Alertness to these issues must extend, therefore, not only within the curatorial side and the director's office but also to any publishing or commercial activities; it is here, where there is any form of commercial or public exploitation, that problems are most likely to arise.

Term of protection

The same as the term of copyright for the relevant work.

What about destruction of an original work such as a painting or manuscript? Can this be a breach?

Destruction in itself cannot be prejudicial to the honour or reputation of the author; however, if the destruction or damage is filmed or the resulting piece is exhibited then this would be of concern and could infringe the right. It is the relationship with the public which is being guarded – not necessarily the safety of the original work.

Example: Following her husband's death, Clementine Churchill burnt Graham Sutherland's portrait of Sir Winston Churchill. Although Sutherland (and the art world) were appalled at the loss of the picture, Lady Churchill justified the act maintaining that her husband had always hated the portrait saying that it made him look 'half-witted'. Such destruction is not to be classified as derogatory treatment – at least under the terms of the current legislation.

Exception   There are various exceptions broadly similar to those set out above for the right of paternity but with more limited exception in relation to reporting current events.

False attribution

The right   A person has the right not to have a literary, dramatic or artistic work falsely attributed to them.

This covers not simply the original work but also any copies. Accordingly, limited edition prints attributed to an artist could be blocked on the grounds that they had not been authorised by the original artist.

How is the right infringed?   The essence of the right is to prevent damage to the author or artist by the public seeing the (unauthorised) work. Accordingly, infringement occurs when the relevant work is published, exhibited publicly, publicly performed or otherwise issued to the public directly or indirectly.

Duration   The lifetime of the author and then a fixed period of 20 years.

Right to privacy

The right   Where a photograph is commissioned for private or domestic purposes, the commissioner (not the photographer) has a limited right of privacy in relation to the work.

The person holding the right has the right not to have the work (or copies of it) issued to the public, exhibited or shown in public or broadcast or included in cable programme service. The main utility of the right is to prevent the publication of private photographs in newspapers or magazines or otherwise exhibited even if the copyright owner (typically the photographer) has given permission for the reproduction.

Exceptions   The right does not apply to photographs or films made prior to 1 August 1989.

There are various exceptions including incidental inclusion in an artistic work, film, broadcast or cable programme.

69

Note: the general fair dealing exceptions do *not* apply in relation to this particular right.

General: consent and waiver

The owners of the relevant moral rights can, of course, consent to the relevant act. Additionally, there can be a more general waiver given by the person entitled to the relevant moral right.

Publication right

Until 1995, the position in relation to out of copyright works was simple.

A work had fallen out of copyright; it was in the public domain. The work could therefore be freely reproduced, without obtaining any prior permission from the author or the current copyright owner and no royalties needed to be paid. The position was certain.

However 1995 saw the introduction of new provisions in relation to extended and revived copyright which threw the position into disarray (see section 2.3). Works by authors such as Virginia Woolf, Rudyard Kipling and James Joyce all came back into copyright or had their terms extended. Even Monet's work came back into copyright briefly.

Conceptually, the justification was that, since these works were subject to the longer periods of protection in various other European countries the term of copyright should be harmonised and, therefore, the extended terms were, effectively, imported from abroad. Apart from photographs (where copyright could have been (and was) revived, in some cases, decades after they had fallen into the public domain), for the most part the discussion surrounded works where the author had died more than 50 years previously but within the preceding 70 years.

However, also as part of the European Commission's determination to harmonise copyright another little known right was brought in which is of great significance to museums and galleries: Publication right.

The rationale for the new right is that a person who first spends time and money in uncovering and communicating to the public an old work which had, previously, fallen out of copyright should be rewarded in some way; they should have a new economic right similar to copyright.

The right is defined as follows: A person who, after the expiry of copyright protection, publishes for the first time a previously unpublished work is given a new property right equivalent to copyright – but without any moral rights.

This seems clear enough. It is essential, however, to look at the exact elements of publication right. The words in the relevant regulations are used unusually and need some consideration.

What types of work are covered?

Literary, dramatic, musical or artistic works or film (but see the comments below relating to literary works).

Note: there is an exclusion in relation to works in relation to which Crown copyright or parliamentary copyright may previously have subsisted.

What is meant by 'previously unpublished'?

Publication, or publishing, are two clear expressions which are generally well understood. However the word 'unpublished' means something different in the specific context of publication right.

For the purposes of the right, 'publication' includes any communication to the public, in particular:

- the issues of copies to the public
- making the work available by means of electronic retrieval system
- the rental or lending of copies of the work to the public
- the performance of the work
- its exhibition or its showing in public
- broadcasting the work, or
- including it in a cable programme service

It should be noted that the Act refers to 'copies' of the work in relation to certain aspects of 'publication': the issue to the public, or rental or lending. It would appear, therefore, that the loan of, for instance, an original manuscript or the sale of an original even to a member of the public, would not precipitate publication for the purposes of publication right.

On the other hand, the performance, exhibition, or showing of the original work, or its broadcast or inclusion in a cable programme service, would constitute publication.

There is an exception: no account shall be taken of any unauthorised act, namely an act done without the consent of the 'owner of the physical medium in which the work is embodied or on which it is recorded'.

Example: Unpublished drawings by John Ruskin awaiting restoration are stolen from the vaults of a university museum. Some years later the drawings turn up at The London Watercolour and Drawings Fair. The showing of the works does not give a publication right to the gallery first exhibiting the works. The acts would have been unauthorised by the true owner. Nor would the 'publication' of a work give the right to the publisher if this were prohibited by, for instance, a specific copyright or location filming agreement entered into with the museum or gallery.

The work must first be published after the expiry of copyright protection

This raises the immediate question: is it necessary for the work, at some stage in the past, to have had copyright protection? What is the position in relation to old artefacts which existed prior to any relevant form of copyright protection? No copyright subsists now; can it be said that copyright has expired?

71

We know, for instance, that sculptures were only first protected by statute as copyright works from 1814 and paintings, drawings and photographs only since 1862. Sadly, this is a confused area because the UK legislation has to be interpreted in accordance with the relevant international convention which uses slightly different wording.

The major difficulty, however, is that various categories of works may have been protected in some form analogous to copyright either by some form of common law copyright or by some other form of ordinance or monopoly even before the first real copyright act, the Statute of Anne, in 1709.

There have been reported 'copyright' cases going back at least until the sixth century. St Columba, for instance, made a manuscript copy of a Psalter belonging to the abbot of a monastery without the abbot's consent. Complaint was made and St Columba ordered to make a payment. Commentators see this as the exercise of a form of copyright. In time, various controls were introduced on printing, charters of the Star Chamber and decrees and ordinances of the Stationers' Company which provided for payment in relation to printed copies of books.

However it is considered that current usage of the word 'copyright' specifically refers to copyright subsisting in accordance with current legislation, namely, the Copyright Designs and Patents Act 1988, in other words statutory copyright. The previous common law copyright was sometime called 'quasi-copyright' or 'the right to restrain publication at common law'. These expressions do not seem to sit happily (or at all) within the definition of copyright as set out in the 1988 Act and the relevant regulations which introduced publication right. So it is possible that for publication right to subsist, the work must have formerly been protected by the modern form of copyright established by statute over the last 300 years.

Categories of work which have, at some time, enjoyed copyright protection

This is a general guide (but the status of individual works will need to be checked in every case):

1 Paintings, graphic works and photographs originated by an author who died after 1855 provided that the work had not been sold or disposed of prior to commencement of the Fine Art Copyright Act 1862

2 Sculptures originated by an artist who died after 1 July 1862

3 Works of artistic craftsmanship created after 1 July 1862

4 Unpublished literary works irrespective of when they were created or when the writer died

5 Unpublished dramatic works irrespective of when they were written or when the playwright died

6 Unpublished musical works irrespective of when they were written or when the composer died

7 British films whenever created

Foreign works   The position in relation to foreign authors and whether their works were, formerly, the subject of copyright protection in the United Kingdom is a complicated area. The position will depend on the country to which the author had a connection and whether work was made before or after 1912.

The former copyright must have expired

There was, formerly, a perpetual copyright in relation to unpublished literary, dramatic, musical works and engravings. Current legislation however introduces what is effectively a long stop date (depending on circumstances) of between 2039 and 2055. By reason of this, it is probable, for the time being at least, there are no opportunities for museums or galleries to secure publication right for these categories of unpublished works.

Of more immediate relevance to the museums and galleries community are the following categories:

- unpublished paintings
- unpublished drawings
- unpublished photographs
- unpublished sculptures
- unpublished works of artistic craftsmanship

The nature of the right

Publication right is an economic right which, to all intents and purposes, is equivalent to copyright. The major difference is that there are no corresponding moral rights like copyright:

- the owner of the right can grant or withhold permission for the reproduction of the relevant work
- the right can be bought or sold
- royalties can be requested
- conditions can be placed on any licence

There are, however, a number of permitted acts; these are, for the most part identical to those in relation to copyright: see section 2.5 above.

How long does publication right last?

Publication right lasts for 25 years from the end of the calendar year in which the work was first published in the way referred to above.

Example: Percy Bysshe Shelley was drowned in a storm in 1822. If a series of poems were now to be discovered and published, the work, as a formerly unpublished literary work, would continue as a copyright *work until the end of the year 2039. Accordingly, publication right could not arise.*

Example: Paul Cézanne died in 1906. His works are currently out of copyright. A large canvas study of an Aix-en-Provence landscape is discovered bricked up in a room in an old farm house. The discovery is first reported by the BBC 9 O'clock News who broadcast the story together with pictures of the painting. The BBC becomes the first owner of the publication right in relation to the picture; it thereby acquires exclusive right for cards, posters and other reproductions. Any person or museum subsequently acquiring the picture at auction will have no rights to reproduce the picture other than via one of the permitted acts or by obtaining the specific consent of the broadcaster.

Example: Inspection by the Rembrandt Research Institute in Amsterdam discloses that some pen and ink drawings thought to be by a later follower of Rembrandt are indeed the work of the master. The drawings are then exhibited at a museum in Wales. The original drawings would never have had copyright protection in this country under the Fine Art Copyright Act 1862. Accordingly, publication right cannot arise nor does any copyright.

One would need to look at the current period of protection (section 2.3 above) to ascertain when copyright in the existing work might have expired. Examples shown at the end of that section also indicate some of the earlier periods of copyright.

Recommendation   Museums and galleries should look very carefully into their archives particularly in relation to lesser known paintings, drawings, photographs and sculptures, which have never been exhibited, included in catalogues or otherwise shown in any way. Potential areas of examination could be artist sketch books, portfolios of unpublished drawings, old wallpaper designs never put into production, maquettes for sculptures never editioned, and prints and negatives of old photographs. Time could usefully be spent considering the works by those artist or creators who died between 1855 and 1929 (being 70 years ago). Of course the position may change – but each year further works do fall out of the ambit of copyright protection. Curators should discuss with any merchandising/commercial arm of their museum or gallery which of those images might be commercially viable.

First ownership of publication right

The first owner of the publication right is the person who first publishes the work – namely, communicates it to the public in the manner set out earlier in this section. There is a danger here. Inadvertently, a museum or gallery might permit a commercial publisher, a researcher, PhD student or indeed anyone having access to the collections to reproduce a relevant work even in some small way. That person (even though they might not realise it) could then become the first publication right owner, not the museum.

Although this might be of limited commercial impact initially, it is critical to understand that this could have very damaging effects on the museum or gallery. If another person becomes the publication right owner then they own all the relevant economic rights to that work. It follows, therefore, that the museum or gallery will be barred from any form of reproduction, publication or exploitation of that work even if they own it. The other person will effectively become a copyright owner; permission would have to be sought and royalties paid. A depressing prospect for the helpful curator.

Publication right is an opportunity for museums and galleries. At last there is the chance for real exclusive rights to be obtained in relation to at least a section of their carefully researched and expensively conserved collections.

3.5 MAKING MONEY – MERCHANDISING AND PUBLISHING

Generally

Here, again, a conflict arises between the duties and responsibilities, both legal and professional, required of museums and galleries to encourage the public to participate freely in the cultural and scientific life of its own community and the importance of self-funding to allow for this. No museum or gallery, whether or not it charges visitors an entrance fee or is in receipt of grants, can avoid thinking about how best to use its collection to increase revenue. The main areas to be considered are merchandising, branding, picture libraries and shops. The latter (shops and restaurants) in reality raise few 'intellectual property rights' issues but there are some general legal issues associated with them which are included for the sake of completeness.

This section also discusses intellectual property rights associated with registered trade marks. These are important rights that are different in nature and scope from copyright.

Merchandising and brands

The Concise Oxford Dictionary (sixth edition) defines 'merchandise' simply as 'goods for sale' and indeed, even in the world of museums and galleries, no narrower definition could be given in view of the variety of items now being produced. Gone are the days when posters, souvenir spoons, mugs and t-shirts were the only items in gallery shops. It is now possible to buy rugs, period clothing, scarves, jewellery, toys, games, maps, stationery and even computer screen savers. Occasionally, it is difficult to see the connection of the goods with the collection, and indeed, there is no obligation for this to be the case. As we shall see however, the mainstays of any merchandising programme are careful choice of goods, suppliers and the exertion of overall control over the process of extracting the 'essence' from items in the collection and incorporating this into an attractive item for sale. The process is likely to involve several types of professional, calling as it does for creative thinking and diligent pursuit of the detail inherent in the development and supply process. Depending on the level of creativity involved, important new rights may be created for the museum body which employs staff; if this creative work is done by external consultants, then a rights transfer is required (see section 3.2).

75

1 Getting started – identifying and clearing rights

In developing a merchandising programme, it is important to examine the rights, if any, which exist in the original object in the collection whose 'essence' or entirety is sought to be reproduced. Any object that was created by an artist who was alive within the last 70 years, or is still alive, should be regarded as 'modern' for copyright purposes. Copyright is likely to subsist in such work, especially if its author was a national of a European Community state (see section 3.4). The right to reproduce the work in any form will therefore need to be cleared with the author or his/her estate. Even simple reproductions such as postcards require this. Obviously, the complexity and expense of the clearance process will depend on the fame of the artist, the perceived desirability of the works and the philosophy of the artist or their estate. Some artists and estates may object to an artist's work being altered or 'treated' in any way. Some artists were known to be very particular about the framing of their works, and estates might argue that removing the frame for the purposes of a postcard is a breach of the artist's moral rights (see section 3.4). In the United Kingdom at least (though not in France), the duration of moral rights is co-extensive with the term for copyright; if the work is out of copyright moral rights will also have lapsed. The two important things to remember are:

- Always clear moral rights in addition to copyright when reproducing for merchandising purposes.

- It is possible for the copyright and moral rights to be owned by different people. While moral rights will always be owned by the artist or the estate, copyright may well have been transferred either by way of sale to a third party publisher or under a will to a beneficiary from the estate.

Similar clearance considerations will apply to the work of any external designer employed to bring additional design features to an article. For example, if a designer designs an unusual clock shape, the face of which bears a form of reproduction of a Salvador Dali clock, rights in both the Dali face and the general clock design must be cleared.

2 Producing the goods and developing the brand

Once the prototype item has been designed, it must then be manufactured. Quality control over the production and manufacturing process is extremely important, not merely for the sake of the goods themselves, but in order to develop or enhance the 'brand' of the museum or gallery. Brands are an increasingly important commercial tool in all forms of trading. In a world of 'information overload', brands are a short form of expression which summarise the message, philosophy, theme, type and general quality of the goods or services supplied under the brand. Brands appear to tell the consumer who is responsible for the product. Because the diversity of products means that the brand owner will rarely actually be responsible for the product manufacture, the exertion of direct or indirect control over the manufacturer is important if the brand message is to remain consistent and representative. As for the brand message to be given by museums and galleries, these will be as different as the institutions themselves. While one museum may wish to convey a message of a lost old-world luxury, another may identify with Warhol 'Pop' commercial culture.

76

No doubt some brand theorists would argue that it is possible for the public to develop inadvertently a notion of a unified 'museum/gallery shop' brand. If this happens in an uncontrolled fashion, the weaknesses of one gallery's merchandise could reflect on those of others.

3   *Legally protecting brands – registered trade marks*

Registered trade marks are the best form of intellectual property right available to protect the brand name or logo of a museum or gallery. A registrable trade mark is any sign capable of being represented graphically (including textually) and which is capable of distinguishing goods or services of one undertaking from those of other undertakings. In order to be effective, a registration process must be undertaken, usually by lawyers or trade mark agents, with attendant costs. Because intellectual property rights are territorially based (see section 2.1) another factor that contributes towards costs is the fact that a trade mark may need to be registered for each geographical territory in which the goods are sold, and in each individual category of goods on which it is used for protection to exist. A schedule of the broad legal categories for which marks can be registered appears in the Appendices (p. 140).

Not all forms of brand may be registered easily and a few not at all. Generally speaking however, if time and money is no object (!), most forms of brands can these days achieve registration in the United Kingdom, provided they have and are being put to substantial use. Registered trade marks can be used to prevent others from adopting the same or a similar brand, and are useful to protect against unauthorised use by counterfeit vendors or even suppliers. They are also useful in connection with merchandising agreements, especially where a number of sub-licences are involved; for example if a merchandising agent is appointed and it then appoints specific product developers who in turn appoint manufacturers. Manufacturers may be located in countries in which there are lower levels of protection for intellectual property rights and any production of goods that is not directly controlled entails a risk of counterfeiting. UK trade mark registrations can prevent unauthorised branded products from being imported back into this country.

Particular advantages associated with registered trade marks include the following:

- Unlike copyright, it is rarely difficult to establish who owns particular marks for the purposes of enforcement; all that is required is to check the register.

- A registered mark can be kept indefinitely provided a renewal fee (every 10 years in the UK) is paid, unlike copyright, which is limited in time.

The main disadvantages are:

- The costs associated with registering; and

- The fact that the rights are purely jurisdictionally based. A registered trade mark in the UK does not prevent mis-use of the brand in the USA unless a further registration is sought there. Again, further costs are involved.

Given the increasing importance of brands and merchandising, it is likely however that registered trade marks will be of increasing significance, particularly if valuable brands are built by virtue of good quality merchandising programmes.

77

Picture libraries

1   *Generally*

Many museums and galleries operate picture libraries, either directly through their own operations, or indirectly using specialist art library houses. The clearance and management of rights is essential to such a business, not least because the rights involved are quite complex. Because of the complexity, the use of specialist art libraries is certainly worth considering. This usually involves the gallery giving a form of exclusive licence to the art library to deal in the gallery's transparencies or indeed to create it own transparencies of the gallery's works (see section 3.1 on filming). Although fees are payable (or a share of income derived from use of the transparencies is deducted), given the increasing emphasis on ownership of rights amongst the art world generally and the difficulties associated with the ease of electronic reproduction, professional management of a gallery's transparencies may be sensible where the resources, time and skills within the gallery itself are limited. It all depends on the nature of the agreement with the specialist. The terms of such an agreement are considered below 'in reverse', that is where it is the gallery as the skilled professional which is taking the exclusive licence. It is also considered in the section on electronic rights and the Internet (section 3.6) where a gallery may decide to sub-license only its electronic rights to a specialist, rather than all rights.

One of the reasons for the complexity of rights management in this area is that there is in fact considerable legal debate as to the nature and extent of rights in transparencies where they are essentially no more than a highly accurate reproduction of an underlying work of art. As has been made clear in other sections of this work (see section 2.2), the copyright in the underlying original artistic work is not the same as any rights in the gallery's reproductions of such works (see section 2.4 on employees and section 3.1 on photographers). The relevant rights in the reproductions, if any, will be those of copyright in photographs. Copyright laws require that photographs be 'original' for copyright to subsist. Originality is arguably lacking when the photograph is a 'mere copy', however accurate and good a copy it is. Under UK law however (though not the copyright law of all countries), it is also clear that copyright will vest in works where skill and labour have been spent in production of the work. Most professional photographers agree that considerable skill and labour goes into the making of high quality transparencies. It is not difficult to appreciate the difference in quality and type of photograph taken by a member of the public using a 'point and click' camera and that taken by professionals for use in commercial reproductions. Without the skill of the professional, the successful communication of the full beauty of the underlying work, by print and other means, is impossible, and few in the industry deny that the creation of a new work, different in form, medium, substance and purpose, has been created. Theoretical legal support for this can also be found, though it is probable that the width of the rights controlled by the 'new' copyright in the transparency would not be as wide as those granted to highly original works of art.

2   *Rights management*

Assuming that a gallery has its own transparencies and wishes to manage the rights in the transparencies, the following are some of the issues which require consideration. Similar considerations (though not identical) will apply to the management of rights in the original art work itself where rights derive directly from the artist or the estate of the artist, though different terms of copyright can apply for artistic works which are not transparencies or photographs (see section 3.4).

An assessment should be made of how much of the collection, in terms of the original art works, remains in copyright and who owns it. Where the underlying work is in copyright, the artist or the estate and/or the copyright owner (if different) will have rights that must be cleared before the gallery can proceed to create or deal in reproductions. There may be exceptions to this rule for certain specific UK galleries whose duties are laid down by statute, but generally speaking, galleries have no rights in underlying copyright unless expressly authorised by the copyright owner.

A similar process should be undertaken in respect of the probable copyright in transparencies, which should be owned by the museum or gallery where full-time employees of the gallery have done the photography in the course of their employment (see sections 3.1 and 2.6). Even where the gallery is confident that it owns copyright in the transparency, it is good practice to keep full details of the actual photographer, including dates of birth and death, the date the photograph was made, and date and place of first publication. ('Publication' for these purposes does not include exhibition, unless the photographer is unknown, where it does.) If the photographer was an employee of another, the details of employment and employer will be required, particularly if the contract dealt with ownership of copyright. If the museum or gallery itself commissioned the taking of the transparencies, details of the commissioning agreement will also be required.

Collecting this information is often difficult and time consuming and may be impossible in cases where records have not been kept or have been lost. Nevertheless, these are the technical details which may need to be established if copyright in any particular transparency is breached and some form of legal action is desired. This is because the term of copyright can depend on several factors, including the 'life of the author, plus 70 years' rule, 50 years from date of publication for certain photographs, or 70 years from the date of being made available to the public where the photographer is unknown. Different rules again apply to unpublished photographs. Working out the exact term of copyright is a complex business (see section 3.4 for further detail) and it is wise to seek expert advice here. Even if it is impossible to reconstruct old records, new information procedures should be established for the photographing of new works, or re-photographing of old.

3 'Rights coming in to the picture library'

This section considers picture library acquisition of rights from a donor owning copyright or where the library otherwise seeks rights regarding original artwork from the copyright owner. General reference should also be made to section 3.3. What follows is a rough checklist for dealing with copyright owners, though achieving it is not always possible. Especially where dealing with artists and estates however, it is important to try and establish mutual trust, so seek to take into account any idiosyncrasies associated with the works or special permission requirements, for example, to always include the frame when reproducing the picture within it. The following guidelines are an attempt at 'reasonable' solutions, rather than seeking a 'one-way commercial advantage' for the library. Specific 'electronic' issues are considered in section 3.6.

- Take a full assignment or exclusive licence if possible. This may not be possible where other licensees of the work already exist;

- Ensure there is a limited term or 'rights reversion' clause for fairness;

- Take extensive rights, including electronic, rental and lending if your library is set up to manage such rights;

- If you take electronic rights, the territory should be world wide in order to deal with possible use on the Internet (see section 3.6 on electronic licensing);

- Agree the share of income or fixed fee to go to the copyright owner and be clear about any deductions that might wish to be made from 'received income' such as VAT and bad debts;

- Agree that the gallery has sole discretion in setting prices to the end-user; it may want to set reduced fees for educational or charitable users;

- Agree periods for rendering accounts – quarterly is usual;

- Include any reasonable notices that the owner may wish to go on reproductions, including copyright notices;

- Agree to allow the owner, especially if the artist or estate is involved, to 'pre-approve' certain uses, using a 'deemed approval' basis after a certain time for consideration;

- Most importantly, seek specific warranties and an indemnity concerning copyright ownership and make enquiries as to the copyright 'chain of title' if unsure.

4 'Rights "going out" from the library'

Take heed of the old maxim 'license in widely and out narrowly'. Having obtained (hopefully), fairly generous rights from the copyright owner, care should be taken to license out those rights fairly narrowly and specifically. This section looks at some general issues, while issues specific to electronic licences, both CD-ROM (and/or other 'physical' platforms) and on-line are considered in section 3.6. Again, a rough 'checklist' of issues follows.

- Ensure that the image names, the territory, language and print run (with room for percentage error) are specifically agreed;

- Discuss exclusivity; ideally the licence should be non-exclusive and exclusive licences in respect of simple works are rare;

- Define the ways in which images may be made available by the library (as opposed to used by the licensee). It may be by transparency, photograph or other forms from which copies may be duplicated. Allow the library to keep supply options open and be able to take advantage of new technologies. Make it clear that there is no obligation to supply the original artwork;

80

- Limit the time for which the images may be held and always provide for their return. Original transparencies can be costly to replace. Consider insuring the transparencies generally and while in transit;

- Many libraries supply their collection in transparent sealed envelopes to enable assessment by the customer before use. Use of the transparent (and therefore an obligation to make payment) should be deemed if the seal has been removed when the original is returned;

- Reserve the right, especially with new customers, to check reproductions before printing commences to ensure quality standards are kept high; this may be required by the copyright owner of the original work. Make it clear from the start whether any special conditions relating to the nature of the reproduction apply; for example whether 'details' are allowed or whether cropping or cutting down is permitted;

- Reserve the libraries' position in respect of sales to public libraries (especially where use is not book related, such as multimedia) unless the gallery has 'lending' rights in connection with the original work;

- Insist on appropriate copyright markings;

- Control the uses of the museum or gallery name and/or logo;

- Be wary of offering too much in the way of guarantees as to copyright ownership, unless the legal position has been checked.

Shops and retail outlets

Generally, retailing is not as exposed from a copyright perspective as is the business of running a licensing based business such as a picture library. Nevertheless, a retailer can be prevented from selling an infringing product and if genuine warnings from a rights-owner are not heeded, may be prevented from selling, made liable for damages and even made subject to criminal provisions. This issue is best handled by dealing only with reputable suppliers and by requiring, usually by way of standard conditions of purchase, guarantees that all rights have been cleared and that no third party could interfere with the sale or use of the product by the retailer or its customers. If letters are received warning that specified products may be infringing copies, prompt action should be taken to investigate the claims.

The other issue of which to be aware when retailing, is that special rights may be required in the product if it is to be put to uses which are separately controlled by intellectual property rights. These include making the items available for rental or lending (e.g. through public libraries) or making them available electronically to users. The latter does not include mere 'e-mail order' over the Internet, although rights may well be required in order to advertise electronically, especially if copies of the products appear. If the gallery has plans to sell in this way, it should make them known to the supplier so that exclusive territorial rights are not granted to other parties.

3.6 THE VIRTUAL MUSEUM – THE INTERNET, THE WORLD WIDE WEB AND ELECTRONIC LICENSING

Generally

The Internet and world wide web are now powerful publishing mediums. Despite numerous unresolved issues regarding copyright and liability for Internet publishing generally, many museums and galleries, including some of the world's most well known, have set up their own world wide web sites. These sites are designed to achieve many purposes including providing historical and current information about the museum, details and 'virtual' tours of parts or all of the collection, visitor information, site maps, and membership and donations information. The more sophisticated sites differentiate between the types of visitors to their site and some provide a higher level of information (both in terms of quality and amount) to educational professionals and researchers in the field.

Also on the increase is the extent to which museums are requested to make images of their collections available to third parties under commercial licences. Commercial art publication for 'print on paper' is still rarely done from digital files alone when it involves high quality colour reproductions. However the day when digital filming alone will be sufficient may not be far off. In the meantime, publishing in respect of CD-ROMs for commercial compilations and multi-media works has its own active market, as do electronic image libraries. Academic institutions and indeed museum professionals desire the sharing of information. Making full details of collections available electronically to others in the museum community represents another form of pressure to digitise works, as does the simple *raison d'être* of most museums and galleries to provide their public visitors with the best and most accessible information about the collection. Keeping these pressures in balance is not easy as fulfilment of some necessarily undermines others. Recognising the uneasy tension that exists is however the first step towards resolving it.

The world wide web

Legally, the world wide web presents significant challenges, many of which are currently unresolved. The principal difficulty revolves around the fact that while the web is multinational, laws and legal systems are not, and remain firmly linked to geographical jurisdictions. In the past, only large multinational companies had to concern themselves with these difficulties; now they are the province of every web site publisher. Significant new laws, which are partly the result of international conventions, will eventually impinge upon the operation of the Internet, but at the time of writing, although the likely substance of these laws is becoming clearer, the detail is still far from certain. All that can be done at this stage is to make educated guesses at the likely ramifications for the operators of web sites as they develop both their web skills and policies for dealing with potential legal issues.

There are two general areas to be considered when operating a web site. These are:

1 What are the issues which must be considered in order not to infringe or breach the rights of others?

2 What steps should be taken to ensure that others do not breach rights of the museum?

1   *What are the issues which must be considered in order not to infringe the rights of others?*

The law here is principally concerned with issues faced by any publisher of information on a multinational basis. Major concerns are copyright and other intellectual property rights, but broad consideration also needs to be given to issues of decency (that is, whether the publication offends laws dealing with pornography and obscenity), reputation (laws dealing with defamation) and reliability (laws dealing with misleading or negligent dissemination of information). Many professional publishers are used to dealing with these issues within the confines of their own jurisdiction. It is however compliance with the potential application of the laws of dozens of countries which makes the web publishing task a daunting one. In order to keep a sense of perspective, the exercise should be seen as one of risk assessment and minimisation, rather than elimination.

For example, in terms of 'risk minimisation', a web site may not be intended to be truly international. It is possible to design a site to make it apparent that its principal application is in relation to one or two jurisdictions; for example by accepting payments only in pounds sterling or requiring a national post code. Similarly, it is possible to appeal only to particular jurisdictions by using the language of that jurisdiction; in this respect, English and Spanish language sites are at particular disadvantages given their increasing use as international languages. If however the site is intended to take advantage of the very strength of the Internet and appeal to a wide variety of international customers, then a policy of following at least a 'lowest common denominator' of legal issues should be adopted. The principal areas to be considered are listed below.

Copyright and intellectual property rights   It is the law in the United Kingdom, and should soon be the law in all European Union countries, that the scanning and electronic reproduction of works of art (either directly or indirectly using transparencies or photographs) is an infringement of copyright in those works of art (see section 2.5 generally). This assumes that copyright in the original works of art has not expired (a complex matter – see section 2.3) and/or that there is copyright in the transparencies (as to which, see p. 78).

If copyrights and/or moral rights (see section 3.4) do exist in the underlying works, then these rights must be cleared on a worldwide basis before they are put on the world wide web. Moral rights and identifying the actual owner of the copyright (particularly in old photographs) is not always easy. Of particular significance in the electronic environment is the moral right to object to 'derogatory' treatment. Very little on the Internet is sacred and it is possible for most images to be manipulated to their detriment using electronic programs; indeed, this is no doubt one of the attractions of electronically published material. Modern works, where the artist or their estate is 'active', can either be the best or the worst of allies here; a reasonable compromise when seeking such rights from artists could be for the museum to agree to bear primary responsibility for taking action against commercial (as opposed to private) infringers of the rights. It is important to remember that in many jurisdictions, an express grant of the right to digitise and publish in digital form will be required from the copyright owner. A general right to reproduce and publish, particularly if given before the Internet was a recognised publishing medium, may not carry this extra grant with it. Conversely, it may be possible to argue that where a specific grant of electronic rights has been given in relation to Internet and multimedia platforms, an 'implied licence' exists in respect of the moral rights attached to the work. This could only be the case however if the copyright owner and the author were the same or related entities. Generally speaking, it is unwise to rely on 'implied' licences.

Copyright is not the only intellectual property right to exist on the Internet (although it is one of the most important). Registered and unregistered trade marks (see generally section 3.5) should also be cleared, particularly if an artist is commercially minded and may have taken steps to register their name or signature as a trade mark, in much the same way that well-known fashion designers do so. Implying or suggesting misleading associations or sponsorship with or by other entities or making unauthorised use of the trading get-up of others may also lead to liability for 'passing off'.

Decency and protection of minors   Although not directly pertaining to the main topic of this book, no consideration of Internet publishing would be complete without reference to this issue. It is the area of most concern to national and supranational parliaments (such as the EU) and at the time of writing, there is considerable legislative and 'pre-legislative' activity in respect of it. A flavour of the concerns can be detected in bills passed in the United States (October 1998). These include the Child Online Protection Act which calls for commercial web site operators who offer 'harmful' material to check on visitors' identifications or face serious fines and prison sentences. Another US Act, the Children's Online Privacy Protection Act requires web site operators to obtain parental consent before collecting information from children aged 12 or younger. (Some of these acts may face constitutional challenges from civil libertarian groups in the US. The depth of concern to government however is apparent.)

In the UK, legislation concerning obscenity is contained in the Obscene Publications Acts (1959 and 1964) and the Protection of Children Act 1978, as amended by the Criminal Justice and Public Order Act 1994. A web site operator who facilitates the transmission of an obscene file can be liable as the publisher of the material. There is also an offence of distributing or possessing with a view to distribute (including electronic storage) indecent photographs of a child. It is a defence to show that the material was not examined and that there was no reasonable cause to suspect that its publication would be an offence. This may be a helpful defence for the running of unsupervised electronic 'chat lines' or bulletin boards. It would not assist where the museum was directly involved in placing material on the web.

The European Community has also been active in this area, although its stance is generally less interventionist. It seems likely that while self-regulation will be permitted, compliance with industry codes will be strongly encouraged. These codes include giving warnings to users if a site carries potentially harmful or offensive material. In the UK, at the time of writing, the Internet industry had agreed a code of conduct which can be found on the web site of the Internet Watch Foundation. In practice, if notified by the authorities of the existence of 'indecent' material on the museum's site, it should be removed immediately.

Perhaps the greatest difficulty in this area is the potential for wide cultural differences in the understanding of 'harmful' and 'offensive'. Caution is recommended. In many cultures and sub-cultures, exposing children (who are commonly adept at 'surfing' the Internet) to nudity of any sort can be regarded as potentially harmful. A check of active commercial art sites based in the US shows that 'warnings' now appear before access is given to individual pictures, some of which a sophisticated museum professional would be unlikely to regard as 'harmful' or 'offensive'.

Reputation   This is a technically complex area of the law and specific advice should be taken, particularly if the aims of the site include engaging in criticism, review or satire. The danger is exacerbated if the site has 'chat rooms' which are available for public comment (even if intended for educational and research purposes). In general, care should be taken not to engage in discussions or publish statements (particularly false ones) which are likely to damage the reputation of any person. Although the law in the UK only protects the reputation of the living, this is not the case in all countries. Similarly, although the law in the UK allows publication of true statements, this is not a complete defence in some jurisdictions, where some additional 'public benefit' may also need to be shown.

Complete compliance with these laws can be difficult. There are however lines of defence which are specifically useful in the electronic environment. Although the law is still in a state of flux, in the US there is a distinct trend towards exonerating providers of sites or services where it is clear that no editorial control is being or is able to be exercised over the content. Again, this is useful for 'chat rooms' but not where site content is handled directly by the museum. In the UK, a similar defence exists where the only involvement in publication is the operating or provision of equipment, system or service by means of which the statement is made available in electronic form. Here however it must also be shown that 'reasonable care' has been taken and no reason to believe that the museum's activities were causing or contributing to the publication of defamation existed. A court would consider the volume of material published, the extent of responsibility for content, the decision to publish, the nature and circumstances of publication and previous conduct of the 'editor' of the site. There are obviously fine lines to be drawn here. Deliberately 'turning a blind eye' to material on the site is not likely to be tolerated, while being completely responsible for everything on the site may be unrealistic. A middle road of using reasonable care while encouraging users and parents of users to exercise caution on sensitive parts of the site is recommended.

Reliable information   The laws surrounding how reliable information must be, and the remedies which can be sought in respect of relying on misleading or inaccurate information vary greatly around the world. Many jurisdictions distinguish between the type of damage suffered as a result of reliance. (Where bodily injury is sustained, remedies are likely to be greater that where the injury is purely 'economic'.) Care should be taken to ensure that basic information is accurate and up to date (such as opening hours) and where information is really just a matter of opinion, this should be clear. A disclaimer of responsibility on an 'about' or 'help' page may assist, but is unlikely to be legally effective in all cases.

2 What steps should be taken to ensure that others do not breach rights of the museum?

Once material is made available on an Internet web site, copying such material is relatively easy and inexpensive. There can be little doubt that making available digital files exposes museums to potential losses as remote private and commercial digital copying is currently difficult to police. Copying is no longer the only concern however and the Internet is rapidly spawning more subtle and damaging unfair trade practices including:

- 'false metatagging' – putting false and hidden information behind web site pages in order to attract the attention of search engines and so divert business;

- 'deep linking' – taking the common practice of hyperlinking and using it to link to pages 'deep within' a web site, thus by-passing the home pages of the linked site;

- 'framing' – accessing another's page through a frame which originates from a different site, so making the framed material appear part of the different site.

The following are preventative measures that may be taken to minimise these problems.

Small digital files   Many museums and galleries have concluded that their web sites must feature elements from the collections in order for the sites to be useful, interesting and relevant. Most have chosen to make images available with only limited digital information so that commercial copying, at least, is not facilitated.

Copyright notices and warnings   Because there is an argument that any material deliberately placed on the Internet with the agreement of the copyright owner carries with it an implied licence to copy the work, it is wise to make clear the museum's policy with respect to copying parts of the web site. If no copying is permitted (or copying only with formal permission), this should be stated clearly under an accessible and obvious page referring to copyright. The real difficulties with policing this should be recognised, and it is common for 'one-off' licences to be granted free of charge for private and domestic use only. All forms of commercial use should be expressly prohibited. Similar notices should be given if no links or framing are permitted. 'Surface' links may be expressly permitted (i.e. links to home pages), indeed some electronic picture libraries insist on such a link as an acknowledgement if small files are reproduced on personal, non-commercial web sites.

Encryption   Any discussion about encryption techniques would rapidly become out-dated. There are however several proprietary systems available, including digital watermarking and the use of 'Java' programming. Few are prepared to say that they are infallible. It is likely however that technological means of image protection will be increasingly important and legal reinforcement is being given to the use of such technology. Many countries, in accordance with an international copyright treaty (WIPO Copyright Treaty agreed in Geneva in December 1996) will be introducing laws to outlaw technologies designed to circumvent copyright protection devices.

Registered trade marks   These can be very effective in preventing misuse of museum names and brands in hidden metatags or in hijacked domain names. Indeed, the US domain name authority, Internic, has been prepared to restore hijacked domain names even where the trade mark is registered outside the US.

Vigilance   There can be no substitute for making regular checks of the Internet using a variety of popular search engines to ensure that the name, reputation and collection of the museum or gallery is not under threat. If infringing activity is detected, swift action is necessary, as defences of 'acquiescence' will arise if nothing decisive is done.

Electronic licensing

Section 2.6 considers licensing generally and is entirely applicable to electronic licences. Clearly electronic licensing raises separate issues and the most important are considered here.

Platform and market choice   At least two distinct markets still exist for electronic rights; the two key markets are CD-ROM (and other 'physical' means of delivery such as floppy disk) and on-line. Licence grants should clearly distinguish which right is being granted, or make it clear if both are. Within these markets are a variety of sub-markets and products. Many book publishers will distinguish between 'electronic books' and 'multimedia' and new markets are appearing all the time. Where possible, a licence should be very specific about the nature of the product and market for which rights are given; where that is impossible, a licence should avoid granting 'all electronic rights'. Care should also be taken with granting territorial rights; while language and 'localisation' rights (i.e. complying with local regulatory, labelling and technological restrictions) are still meaningful, territorial rights are difficult to control where actual reproduction on the Internet is involved.

Specific controls on licensee   Allied to the above is the need to limit or control the licensee specifically in respect of certain activities. These should be isolated and the prohibition or control agreed. For example, use of images in connection with a 'service' offered by the licensee may or may not be part of an on-line agreement. Controls on the size of digital files that appear on the Internet are also important in controlling piracy, and the use of specified encryption technology or restricted access in the provision of large files is recommended. For similar reasons, a requirement to reproduce the museum's copyright notices with

87

all copies of the image should also be included. If a licensor is given substantial rights in relation to a collection – either in terms of having access to a large amount of the collection or by virtue of having sole or exclusive rights, it should also be obliged to assist in a meaningful way in the battle against piracy.

Where electronic rights are granted in respect of physical media, controls over the manufacturing site and specific limit on the number of copies produced should be included. Many CD-ROM manufacturing sites exist in countries where lower levels of intellectual property protection exist, and care should be taken by both parties to avoid them.

Controls of end-users One of the major differences between standard and electronic licences is the need in respect of the latter to attempt to control use by end-users. (This form of restriction is not generally permissible in relation to goods which do not involve the user in engaging in acts which would otherwise be infringements of intellectual property right.) The restrictions in the licence will have no direct effect on the user, who is not, after all, a party to the licence with the museum. The restrictions should nevertheless be designed to oblige the licensee to draw to the attention of the end-user certain limitations in the extent of the licences granted. The restrictions often take the form of a 'shrink-wrap' licence, provided by the licensee. The legal validity of 'shrink-wraps' has often been queried but in view of their widespread use, courts in both the UK and US are upholding them. These licences will mostly be designed to protect the rights of the licensee, but they may also include prohibitions against:

- use of the images for any purpose other than strictly private and domestic, and

- use on 'wide or local area networks' including intranets or the Internet itself

4. Appendices

The Kiss by Auguste Rodin (1840–1917) © Tate Gallery, London
Another example of an art photograph, this time of a three-dimensional artistic work. The sculpture will have been protected by copyright but as Rodin died over 70 years ago it has now expired. The copyright in the photograph will expire 70 years after the death of the photographer. In this case the photographer works for the Tate Gallery and so the copyright belongs with the Tate.

4.1 RELEVANT SOURCES, FURTHER READING

The law

This guide is concerned with the law of copyright in the United Kingdom. The law of copyright in the UK is contained in the *Copyright, Designs and Patents Act 1988* (as amended) ('the 1988 Act'), copies of which may be obtained from HMSO. Those regularly involved with copyright may find a copy of the 1988 Act helpful. It should be noted however that, in addition to the 1988 Act:-

(a) rules and regulations made under the 1988 Act are contained in a series of statutory instruments, of which a number are relevant to museums and galleries, such as the Copyright (Libraries and Archivists) (Copying of Copyright Material) Regulations 1989 [S1 1989 No. 1212]; and

(b) as provided in Schedule 1 of the 1988 Act, some provisions of the Copyright Act 1956 and even of the Copyright Act 1911 continue to have effect in relation to older works.

The law of copyright is no different in *Scotland* from any other part of the United Kingdom but the rules on ownership of physical property and court rules, procedures and the remedies available in the event of copyright infringement may differ. An outline of the main differences between Scots Law and that in force in the rest of the United Kingdom is provided in Appendix 4.4. The advice of a Scottish lawyer should certainly be sought in relation to these requests.

It should be noted that the 1988 Act has been *amended* several times in recent years to implement a range of *EC Directives*. If you are consulting the 1988 Act, you must make sure that you are using the 1988 Act *as amended*.

Further reading

There is a vast range of publications on copyright; the following is only a tiny selection:

Museums Association Briefing Notes on Copyright.

Flint, M. *User's Guide to Copyright* (4th edition, 1997), Butterworths.

Copinger & Skone James on Copyright (14th edition, 1999), Sweet & Maxwell.

Whale on Copyright (5th edition, 1997), Sweet & Maxwell.

Henry, M. *Current Copyright Law* (1998), Butterworths.

4.2 RELEVANT BODIES

Museums Copyright Group (MCG), c/o Peter Wienand, Chairman, Farrer & Co., 66 Lincoln's Inn Fields, London WC2A 3LH; tel. 0207 917 7355; e-mail jpw@farrer.co.uk or e-mail emma@pcell.demon.co.uk

Founded in 1996 by a group of museum professionals who felt that the museums sector needed greater representation in the copyright sphere. This guide is an initiative of the MCG.

Museums and Galleries Commission (MGC), 16 Queen Anne's Gate, London SW1H 9AA; tel. 0207 233 4200; fax 0207 233 3686.

This guide has been produced with the generous assistance of the MGC. Contacts: Heather Wilson, David Dawson. The MGC has been replaced by a new body, provisionally entitled the Museums Libraries and Archives Council (MLAC), which became operational on 1 April 2000. MLAC's address and details are Room 545, Grove House, Orange Street, London WC2H 7ED; tel. 0207 211 2028; fax 0207 211 2006; e-mail neville. mackay@culture.gov.uk

Museums Association (MA), 42 Clerkenwell Close, London EC1R 0PA; tel. 0207 608 2933; fax 0207 250 1929.

Publishes the *Briefing Notes on Copyright* and the *Museums Journal* which occasionally carries pieces on copyright.

MDA, Jupiter House, Station Road, Cambridge CB1 2JD; tel. 01223 315760; fax 01223 362521; e-mail mda@mdocassn.demon.co.uk

Considers copyright in the context of its work on information management.

Museum Trading and Publishing Group (MTPG), c/o Rachel Hill, Bodleian Library, Oxford, OX1 3BG; tel. 01865 277000; reh@bodley.ox.ac.uk

Founded 1978 for Museum Publishing and Shop Management; publishes a Newsletter and organises seminars.

Scottish Cultural Resources Access Network (SCRAN), Abden House, 1 Marchhall Crescent, Edinburgh EH16 5HP; tel. 0131 662 1211; fax 0131 662 1511; e-mail b.royan@stir.ac.uk   website http://www.scran.ac.uk

Royal Commission on Historical Manuscripts, Quality House, Quality Court, Charing Lane, London WC2A 1HP; tel. 0207 242 1198; fax 0207 831 3550; e-mail nra@hmc.gov.uk   website http://www.hmc.gov.uk

Library Association 19–29 Woburn Place, London WC1H 0LU; tel. 0207 273 8700; fax 0207 273 8701; e-mail libcom@lic.gov.uk   website: http://www. lic.gov.uk

Public Record Office (PRO), Kew, Richmond, Surrey TW9 4DU; tel. 0208 876 3444; fax 0208 392 5295; e-mail: presspub.pro.kew@gtnet.gov.uk   website http://www.open.gov.uk/gov.uk/pro/prohome.htm

Copyright Officer: Tim Padfield

British Library, Boston Spa, Wetherby, West Yorks LS23 7BQ; tel. 01937 546585; fax 01937 546586; e-mail nbs-info@bl.uk   website http://portico. bl.uk

Publishers Association, 19 Bedford Square, London WC1B 3HJ; tel. 0207 580 6321; fax 0207 636 5375.

The Copyright Licensing Agency Limited (CLA), 88 Tottenham Court Road, London W1P 9HE; tel. 0207 436 5931.

The Newspaper Licensing Agency Limited (NLA), Lonsdale Gate, Lonsdale Gardens, Tunbridge Wells, Kent TN1 1NL; tel. 01892 525273.

The Performing Rights Society Limited (PRS), 29–33 Berners Street, London W1P 4AA; tel. 0207 580 5544.

Phonographic Performance Limited (PPL), 1 Upper James Street, London W1R 3HG; tel. 0207 534 1000.

Mechanical Copyright Protection Society (MCPS), Elgar House, 41 Streatham High Road, London SW16 1ER; tel. 0208 664 4400.

The Design and Artists' Copyright Society Limited (DACS), Parchment House, 13 Northburgh Street, London EC1V 0AH; tel. 0207 336 8811.

4.3 SAMPLE AGREEMENTS FOR DEALINGS IN COPYRIGHT

Caveat

The sample documents which follow are precedents which may be used as a starting point in transactions between museums and users or owners of copyright material. All the documents will need to be altered to suit specific circumstances. Where there is any doubt about a provision contained in one of the documents or concern about altering a document, advice should be sought. The documents are intended to create legally binding rights and obligations which could be affected by any alteration.

Purchasers of this book have a non-exclusive licence to use and reproduce the documents contained in this book for their own internal purposes. This licence does not extend to any further publication whether in printed, electronic or other form. Neither the authors nor the publisher accept any liability for loss arising from using the documents or failing to use them.

PHOTOGRAPHIC IMAGE LICENCE

<table>
<tr>
<td>Permission to reproduce
Requested by:
('the Licensee')</td>
<td colspan="4">Name:

Address:

Tel. No: Fax No:
Email:</td>
</tr>
<tr>
<td rowspan="2">Purpose of reproduction:
('the Purpose')</td>
<td>Advertising/
Promotional</td>
<td colspan="2">Commercial Project</td>
<td>Educational
Project</td>
</tr>
<tr>
<td>Inside
Illustration</td>
<td>Jacket/
Cover</td>
<td>TV Still</td>
<td>Other
(please state)</td>
</tr>
<tr>
<td>Image to be reproduced:
('the Image')</td>
<td>Author</td>
<td>Cat.No</td>
<td colspan="2">Photograph/Transparency</td>
<td>Col or
b/w</td>
</tr>
<tr>
<td>Type of Publication:</td>
<td>Book</td>
<td>Newspaper/
Magazine</td>
<td colspan="2">Record/
Cassette/
CD Cover</td>
<td>Television</td>
<td>Other
(please
state)</td>
</tr>
<tr>
<td>Title of Publication/Programme
('the Publication'):</td>
<td colspan="4"></td>
</tr>
<tr>
<td>Print Run:</td>
<td colspan="2">5,000 or less</td>
<td>5,000–15,000</td>
<td>15,000 or more
(please state)</td>
</tr>
<tr>
<td rowspan="2">Rights Required:
('the Rights')</td>
<td>One language, one
country</td>
<td colspan="2">World Rights, one
language</td>
<td>World Rights,
multiple languages</td>
</tr>
<tr>
<td>Standard TV</td>
<td colspan="2">Non-Standard TV</td>
<td>Other (please
state)</td>
</tr>
<tr>
<td>Approximate Date of Release:</td>
<td colspan="4"></td>
</tr>
<tr>
<td>(For Transparency hire
only) 'the Period of Hire':</td>
<td colspan="4"></td>
</tr>
<tr>
<td colspan="5">In consideration of the Licensee paying the fee of [   ], payable under Clause 11 of this
Agreement ('the Fee') [   ] ('the Museum') hereby agrees that the Licensee may use the
Image upon the terms and conditions contained herein.</td>
</tr>
<tr>
<td>Date:</td>
<td colspan="4"></td>
</tr>
<tr>
<td>Signed for and on
behalf of the Licensee:</td>
<td colspan="4"></td>
</tr>
<tr>
<td>Signed for and on
behalf of the Museum:</td>
<td colspan="4"></td>
</tr>
</table>

TERMS AND CONDITIONS FOR THE REPRODUCTION OF PHOTOGRAPHS AND TRANSPARENCIES

These Terms and Conditions apply to conventional reproduction only. Reproduction in an electronic or multimedia product is subject to separate terms and conditions.

Permission to reproduce is dependent on the full acceptance of the Terms and Conditions detailed below and will be automatically withdrawn should any part be infringed.

1. The Licensee is granted permission to reproduce the Image in the Publication for the Purpose only.

2. The Rights that are granted to the Licensee in respect of the Image are non-exclusive. All reprints, further editions or use of the Image, other than for the Purpose, including reproduction for an increase in the Print Run, necessitate a new application to the Museum and payment of a further fee. This also applies to television programmes where permission to reproduce covers one transmission only.

3. Copyright in the Image remains the property of the Museum unless otherwise stated. Photographs of works of art by living artists or artists who died less than 70 years ago can only be supplied, other than for research and private study, if the Licensee has obtained written consent from the owner of the copyright in the works of art, a copy of which must be sent to the Museum before the Image can be released.

4. The Licensee must satisfy himself that all necessary rights, releases or consents which may be required for reproduction of the Image are obtained, and the Museum gives no warranty or undertaking that any such rights, releases or consents are or will be obtained whether in relation to the use of names, people, trade marks, registered or copyright designs, or works of art depicted in any picture.

5. The Licensee agrees to indemnify the Museum in respect of any claims or damages or any loss or costs arising in any manner from the reproduction without proper rights or consents of any of the Image.

6. The Museum shall not be liable for any loss or damage suffered by the Licensee or by any third party arising from the use of any of the Image.

7. All reproduction of the Image must include the acknowledgement PHOTO-GRAPH REPRODUCED WITH THE KIND PERMISSION OF [   ] along with the name and dates of the creator and the title and date of the work reproduced in the Image or details on the caption supplied.

8. If the Image or any work reproduced in the Image has not previously been published then any publication rights therein are hereby assigned absolutely to the Museum for the full period of such publication rights.

9. No part of the Image may be manipulated, masked out, cut down, superimposed with typed matter, or in any way defaced without prior agreement.

10. Application to reproduce a detail from any work will be considered only upon receipt of a sketch or marked-up photograph, showing the area to be reproduced. The caption must include the word 'DETAIL'.

11. Service fees may be charged to cover administrative costs and despatch of the Image. Licensees will be warned of these charges in advance. Payment of service fees does not give rise to any rights in the Image.

12. The Licensee must pay the Fee payable by reference to the scale of fees set out in the Schedule to this Agreement.

13. Payment of the Fee should be made within 30 days of invoicing. All bank charges must be borne by the Licensee. The Image may not be sent if payment is not received in full.

14. Cheques must be made payable to [   ] in UK pounds sterling.

15. Permission to reproduce the Image will not be granted until the Fee payable has been agreed and paid.

16. No variation of the terms and conditions set out herein shall be effective unless agreed in writing by both parties.

Image Hire

17. Arrangements to hire an Image are subject to its availability. Licensees will be charged if new photography is required, or the urgency of the request requires a new duplicate transparency to be made.

18. The Licensee should note the Period of Hire. Late return will attract an additional fee of £[   ] per week.

19. The Period of Hire will commence on the date of despatch from the Museum and will cease on the date the transparency is received by the Museum.

20. Transparencies must be carefully handled. They are easily damaged by fingerprints and exposure to heat and light. They must be returned:

    (i)   undamaged;

    (ii) in the correct pockets; and

    (iii) free from any substance used to prevent slippage during scanning.

21. It is strictly prohibited to make duplicates of any transparencies supplied by the Museum other than as expressly permitted by the Agreement.

22. Transparencies hired from the Museum are not to be lent, resold, hired out or otherwise circulated without prior permission of the Museum.

23. This Agreement shall be governed by the laws of [England and Wales].

THE SCHEDULE

Reproduction fees

The following fees are for colour and black and white reproductions.

	ONE LANGUAGE, ONE COUNTRY	WORLD RIGHTS, ONE LANGUAGE	WORLD RIGHTS, MULTIPLE LANGUAGES
PUBLICATIONS			
Books, Part works & Periodicals			
Press and Magazine Advertising			
COVERS			
Book & Audio Book jackets & Magazine covers			
CD, Cassette, Record or Video covers (per format)			
MERCHANDISE			
Greeting cards or postcard			
Fine Art prints (up to A4)			
Posters			
Calendars			
STANDARD TELEVISION (Standard, cable or satellite – per format)			
On time flash fee up to 30 seconds			
As above – Educational			
Video			
Video – Educational			

The fees for non-standard television and other types of right are negotiable.

These fees do not include any copyright fees due to an artist or to the estate of an artist whose work is in copyright.

These fees do not include any service fee payable under clause 11.

VAT AT 17½% WILL BE CHARGED, WHERE APPLICABLE, IN ADDITION TO THESE FEES.

If clients are requesting a discount for educational, non-profitmaking use, they should provide full details of the project including funding and relevant documentation.

FILM/AUDIO VISUAL MATERIAL LICENCE

Permission to reproduce Requested by: ('the Licensee')	Name: Address: Tel. No: Fax No: Email:			
Purpose of reproduction: ('the Purpose')	Advertising/ Promotional		Commercial Project	
	Record/ Cassette/ CD	Television/ Video	Film	Other (please state)
Material to be reproduced: ('the Material')	Author	Cat.No		Film
Title of work ('the Work'):				
Rights Required: ('the Rights')	One language, one country	World Rights, one language	World Rights, multiple languages	
	Standard TV	Non-Standard TV	Other (please state)	
Period of Hire:	to			
Approximate Date of Release:				
In consideration of the Licensee paying the fee of [ ], payable under Clause 14 of this Agreement ('the Fee') [ ] ('the Museum') hereby agrees that the Licensee may use the Material upon the terms and conditions contained herein.				
Date:				
Signed for and on behalf of the Licensee:				
Signed for and on behalf of the Museum:				

TERMS AND CONDITIONS FOR THE REPRODUCTION OF FILM AND VISUAL MATERIAL

These Terms and Conditions apply to conventional reproduction only. Reproduction in an electronic or multimedia product is subject to separate terms and conditions.

Permission to reproduce is dependent on the full acceptance of the Terms and Conditions detailed below and will be automatically withdrawn should any part be infringed.

1. The Licensee is granted permission to reproduce the Material in the Work for the Purpose only.

2. The Rights that are granted to the Licensee in respect of the Material are non-exclusive. All further releases or uses of the Material, other than for the Purpose, necessitate a new application to the Museum and payment of a further fee. This also applies to television programmes where permission to reproduce covers one transmission only.

3. Works by living directors, authors or composers, or directors, authors or composers, the last of whom died less than 70 years ago can only be supplied, other than for research and private study, if the Licensee has obtained written consent from the owner of the copyright, a copy of which must be sent to the Museum before the Material can be released.

4. The Licensee must satisfy himself that all necessary rights, releases or consents which may be required for reproduction of the Material are obtained, and the Museum gives no warranty or undertaking that any such rights, releases or consents are or will be obtained whether in relation to the use of names, people, trade marks, registered or copyright designs, or works of art depicted in any work.

5. Where the copyright holder or owner is known, the Licensee shall provide the Museum with the copyright holder's or owner's written permission for the release of the Material.

6. Where the copyright holder or owner is not known and the Museum is satisfied that every reasonable effort has been made to find him, the Licensee accepts the responsibility for clearance of all rights and payment of fees that may become due as a result of exhibiting the Material and agrees to indemnify the Museum against any liability it might incur in respect of the reproduction of the Material.

7. Where music and performers' rights are involved the Museum can give no warranties as to ownership of these rights and it is the responsibility of the Licensee to obtain all necessary clearances and consents.

8. The Licensee agrees to indemnify the Museum in respect of any claims or damages or any loss or costs arising in any manner from the reproduction without proper rights or consents of any of the Materials.

9. The Museum shall not be liable for any loss or damage suffered by the Licensee or by any third party arising from the use of any of the Materials.

10. The Use of the Materials must include the acknowledgement REPRODUCED WITH THE KIND PERMISSION OF [   ] along with the name and dates of the creator and the title and date of the Material or details on the caption supplied.

11. If the Material or any work appearing or embodied in the Material has not previously been published then any publication rights therein are hereby assigned absolutely to the Museum for the full period of such publication rights.

12. No part of the Material may be manipulated, altered, superimposed with other material, or in any way defaced without prior agreement.

13. Service fees may be charged to cover administrative costs and despatch of the Material. Licensees will be warned of these charges in advance. Payment of service fees does not give rise to any rights in the Material.

14. The Licensee must pay the Fee payable by reference to the scale of fees set out in the Schedule to this Agreement.

15. Payment of the Fee should be made within 30 days of invoicing. All bank charges must be borne by the Licensee. The Material may not be sent if payment is not received in full.

16. Cheques must be made payable to [   ] in UK pounds sterling.

17. Permission to reproduce the Material will not be granted until the Fee payable has been agreed.

18. No variation of terms and conditions set out herein shall be effective unless agreed in writing by both parties.

19. Arrangements to hire film are subject to its availability. Licensees will be charged if further photography, recording or filming is required, or the urgency of the request requires a new duplicate film to be made.

20. The Licensee should note the Period of Hire. Late return will attract an additional fee of £[   ] per week.

21. The Period of Hire will commence on the date of despatch from the Museum and will cease on the date the Material is received by the Museum.

22. Films must be carefully handled. They are easily damaged by fingerprints and exposure to heat and light. They must be returned undamaged and in the correct pockets.

23. It is strictly prohibited to make duplicates of any of the Material.

24. Save as provided in this Agreement films hired from the Museum are not to be lent, resold, hired out or otherwise circulated without prior permission of the Museum.

25. The Museum reserves the right to acquire free of charge, on demand, a viewing copy of the finished Work.

26. This Agreement shall be governed by the laws of [England and Wales].

THE SCHEDULE

Reproduction fees

The following fees are for colour and black and white reproductions.

	ONE LANGUAGE, ONE COUNTRY	WORLD RIGHTS, ONE LANGUAGE	WORLD RIGHTS, MULTIPLE LANGUAGES
STANDARD TELEVISION (Standard, cable or satellite – per format)			
On time flash fee up to 30 seconds			
STANDARD VIDEO			
On time flash fee up to 30 seconds			
As above – Educational			
CINEMA RELEASE			
On time flash fee up to 30 seconds			

The fees for non-standard television, video and cinema release and other types of right are negotiable.

These fees do not include any fees due to third party copyright owners or performers under clauses 3–7 of this Agreement.

These fees do not include any service fee payable under clause 13.

VAT AT 17½% WILL BE CHARGED, WHERE APPLICABLE, IN ADDITION TO THESE FEES.

If clients are requesting a discount for educational, non-profitmaking use, they should provide full details of the project including funding and relevant documentation.

LICENCE FOR THE ELECTRONIC USE OF IMAGES (ON-LINE)

Licensee:	
Licensee's address:	
Images: (being photographs of works in the Museum's collection)	
Website or other details:	
The Term:	
Licence Fee per Image:	(plus VAT if applicable) Total Fee:

Signed for and on behalf of the Museum: _____
Date: _____

Signed for and on behalf of the Licensee: _____
Date: _____

This licence is governed by the terms set out overleaf which may not be altered in any particular without written consent of the Museum.

TERMS AND CONDITIONS FOR THE ELECTRONIC USE OF IMAGES (ON-LINE)

1. [   ] ('the Museum') agrees to grant to the person or company named overleaf ('the Licensee') a non-exclusive licence in the territory specified overleaf to scan the photographic images described overleaf ('the Images') onto an electronic database under the Licensee's control for the sole purpose of allowing the Images to be viewed on the website specified overleaf ('the Website') for the term specified overleaf.

2. This licence is granted subject to the following conditions:

   (a) no re-use or further reproduction of the Images is permitted except on payment in advance of additional fees;

   (b) no copy of the Images shall be of any greater resolution than [640 × 480] pixel resolution;

   (c) the Licensee may not copy any version of the Images other than the transparencies or other versions delivered by the Museum for the purpose. Any such original transparencies or other versions of the Images shall be returned to the Museum no later than 5 working days after they have been recorded by the Licensee pursuant to 1(a) above. The Licensee shall be fully liable for any loss or damage to such transparencies or versions while they are in the Licensee's possession or control;

   (d) the Licensee shall encrypt the digitised Images using an agreed unique encryption code or watermark which is traceable on all copies;

   (e) the Licensee hereby assigns the entire copyright and any similar rights throughout the world in any digitisation of the Images created by or for the Licensee for the full term of such copyright and similar rights including extensions and renewals;

   (f) if the Images or any work reproduced in the Images have not previously been published then any publication rights therein are hereby assigned absolutely to the Museum for the full period of such publication rights;

   (g) the Licensee warrants that it has or shall have obtained all necessary permissions from the owner of any copyright in the work recorded in the Image and indemnifies the Museum against all costs, damages and expenses which the Museum may incur as a result of failure to obtain such permissions;

   (h) all displays of the Images on screen shall be accompanied by (i) a copyright notice prohibiting any form of reproduction, transmission, performance, display, rental, lending or storage in any retrieval system without the consent of the copyright holders; and (ii) a credit acknowledging that the Images have been used with the permission of the Museum, such credit to be of a size and in a place to be agreed; and (iii) a credit in a form to be agreed identifying the author of the Images;

   (i) on expiry of the Term all copies or records of the Images made under this licence shall be erased from the Licensee's database and a certificate provided to the Museum to that effect, unless a further production run is agreed and the relevant additional fees paid;

(*A Guide to Copyright for Museums and Galleries*, Routledge: 2000)

(j) no adaptation, alteration or manipulation whatsoever of any of the Images is permitted without the prior written consent of the Museum;

(k) the licence may not be assigned, transferred or sub-licensed without the prior written consent of the Museum; and

(l) the Licensee shall inform the Museum of any unauthorised use in any of the Images as soon as it becomes aware of the same.

3. In consideration of this licence, the Licensee shall pay the Museum the licence fee set out overleaf. The licence fee applies to this licence only. The said sum is exclusive of VAT which shall be payable in addition at the rate and in the manner prescribed by law. The licence fee shall be payable prior to delivery of the Images to the Licensee. The licence fee does not include print fees and hire charges, which may be invoiced by the Museum in addition.

4. This licence may be revoked at any time if the Licensee is in breach of any of its terms.

5. This licence shall be governed by the laws of [England and Wales].

LICENCE FOR THE ELECTRONIC USE OF IMAGES (OFF-LINE)

Licensee:	
Licensee's address:	
Images: (being photographs of works in the Museum's collection)	
The Product:	Nature of Product (i.e. CD-ROM, CDi, other): Title:
The Production Run:	Units
The Territory:	
Website:	
The Term:	
Licence Fee per Image:	(plus VAT if applicable) Total Fee:
Royalty:	% of the Licensee's approved retail price at which each copy of the Product is sold in the Territory

Signed for and on behalf of the Museum: _____
Date: _____

Signed for and on behalf of the Licensee: _____
Date: _____

This licence is governed by the terms set out overleaf which may not be altered in any particular without written consent of the Museum.

TERMS AND CONDITIONS FOR THE ELECTRONIC USE OF IMAGES
(OFF-LINE)

1. [   ] ('the Museum') agrees to grant a non-exclusive licence in the territory specified overleaf to the person or company named overleaf ('the Licensee'):

   (a) to record and hold the photographic images described overleaf ('the Images') on an electronic database under the Licensee's control;

   (b) to reproduce the Images once on the electronic product described overleaf ('the Product'); and

   (c) to reproduce no more than one Image for the purposes of advertising the Product on the website specified overleaf

   until expiry of the Term or until the production run specified overleaf is completed, whichever occurs soonest.

2. This licence is granted subject to the following conditions:

   (a) no re-use or further reproduction of the Images whether for future production runs or otherwise is permitted except on payment in advance of additional fees;

   (b) no copy of the Images shall be of any greater resolution than [640 × 480] pixel resolution except for the Image reproduced on the website specified overleaf which shall be of 'thumb-nail' resolution only (i.e. [×   ] pixel);

   (c) the Licensee may not copy any version of the Images other than the transparencies or other versions delivered by the Museum for the purpose. Any such original transparencies or other versions of the Images shall be returned to the Museum no later than 5 working days after they have been recorded by the Licensee pursuant to 1(a) above. The Licensee shall be fully liable for any loss or damage to such transparencies or versions while they are in the Licensee's possession or control;

   (d) the Licensee shall encrypt the digitised Images using an agreed encryption code or watermark unique to the Product which is traceable on all copies;

   (e) the Licensee hereby assigns any copyright and similar rights throughout the world in any digitisation of the Images created by or for the Licensee for the full term of such copyright and similar rights including extensions and renewals;

   (f) if the Images or any works reproduced in the Images have not previously been published then any publication right therein is hereby assigned absolutely to the Museum for the full period of such publication rights;

   (g) the Licensee warrants that it has or shall have obtained all necessary permissions from the owner of any copyright in the work recorded in the Image and indemnifies the Museum against all costs, damages and expenses which the Museum may incur as a result of failure to obtain such permissions;

   (h) all copies of the Product and its packaging and any accessible displays of the Images on screen shall be accompanied by (i) a copyright notice prohibiting any form of reproduction, transmission, performance, display, rental, lending or storage in any retrieval system without the consent of the copyright holders; and (ii) a credit acknowledging that the Images have been used with the permission of the Museum, such credit to be of a size and in a place to be agreed; and (iii) a credit in a form to be agreed identifying the author of the Images;

(i) at least two copies of the Product shall be given to the Museum free of charge following publication;

(j) on completion of the production run specified overleaf all copies or records of the Images made under this licence shall be erased from the Licensee's database and a certificate provided to the Museum to that effect, unless a further production run is agreed and the relevant additional fees paid;

(k) no adaptation, alteration or manipulation whatsoever of any of the Images is permitted without the prior written consent of the Museum;

(l) the licence may not be assigned, transferred or sub-licensed without the prior written consent of the Museum;

(m) the Licensee shall ensure that third parties including distributors are bound by the terms of this licence; and

(n) the Licensee shall inform the Museum of any unauthorised use in any of the Images as soon as it becomes aware of the same.

3. In consideration of this licence, the Licensee shall pay the Museum the licence fee and the royalties set out overleaf. The licence fee and royalties apply to this licence only. The said sums are exclusive of VAT which shall be payable in addition at the rate and in the manner prescribed by law. The licence fee shall be payable prior to delivery of the Images to the Licensee. Where royalties are due the Licensee shall within 30 days of each quarter day provide an account of the amount due in respect of the quarter ending on that quarter day and shall pay the said amount within 30 days of the Museum's invoice therefor. The licence fee and royalties do not include print fees and hire charges, which may be invoiced by the Museum in addition.

4. This licence may be revoked at any time if the Licensee is in breach of any of its terms.

5. This licence shall be governed by the laws of [England and Wales].

PHOTOGRAPHY COMMISSION CONTRACT

[Buy-Out Of All Rights]

To: [name of photographer]	
This is to confirm the commission of photography from you. The proposed arrangements are as follows:	
Location of Shoot:	[ ] Gallery/Building
Objects to be Photographed:	[describe]
Number of Photographs Required:	[All film? or specify number required]
Dates of Shoot:	[dates]
Format of Film:	[specify site/format: colour/black and white/digital etc]
Fee:	[specify day rate or fixed fee] [+ VAT?]
Expenses to be paid by Photographer:	[specify travel, equipment hire, lighting, hire, styling etc]
Expenses to be paid by the Museum:	[film stock at cost (plus 10%?)] [processing charges] [Courier charges at cost:] [Contact Sheets] [Black and White prints] [specify]
Designated Officer:	[state name of person/curator giving brief to, and supervising the Photographer]
Credit: 'Photography by [photographer]' [delete if inapplicable].	

1. We commission you to carry out the photography in accordance with the Details as set out above. You will supply your own equipment and the only expenses that the Museum will bear are those specified as payable by us in the Details section.

2. You will comply with the 'Guidelines for the Photography' as issued by the Museum from time to time.

   [Note: it would be useful for the Museum to have prepared basic guidelines for persons having access to the collections such as hours of access, parking arrangements, security badges, lighting, cables, fire precautions, smoking etc].

3. In consideration for the payment by the Museum of the Fee, you:

- will deliver to us all negatives, transparencies, digital files and other photographic material taken at the Location or elsewhere at the Museum whether or not of the Objects ('the Photographic Material')

- hereby assign to [the Trustees of the Museum (specify exactly)] all and any copyright, world-wide, together with any renewals and extensions thereof in the Photographic Material

- hereby assign to [the Trustee of the Museum] all and any publication right which may arise by reason of the publication or communication to the public of any work depicted within the Photographic Material

4. You undertake that you will be the author of all the Photographic Material, that you are able to enter into this agreement and assign the rights to us as set out above.

5. You undertake that of the Photographic Material at least [specify number] of the photograph will be of high professional quality suitable for reproduction by the Museum for the proposed usage, in accordance with the brief given to you by the Designated Officer.

6. You undertake to obtain signed Model Release forms from any people featured in the images you have created.

7. You further undertake not to keep or retain any out-takes or other parts of the Photographic Material for your own purposes or for sale, assignment or licensing to anyone else.

   [We agree, however, that up to [specify number] of the photographic images may be used by you for (example as follows) the purposes of self promotion namely on A5 size photographic cards within photographic directories or on any website published by you or any such directory provided that any use on a website shall be on the basis that the images are of low resolution and cannot be downloaded by third parties.]

   Any such use shall be conditional upon the following credit being given ('© ....).

8. We shall own the physical property in the Photographic Material or Digital Files.

9. English law shall apply.

10. Any variation to this agreement shall be in writing signed by us both. If you agree to the terms of this commission, I would be grateful if you could sign and return to me the attached copy of the letter.

Signed ....

Duly authorised for and on behalf of [the Museum]

I accept the terms as set out above.

Signed ....

The Photographer

PERMISSION FOR PHOTOGRAPHY IN THE GALLERY

[   ] Museum

Photography Agreement

Parties:	[Museum] ('the Museum') [address].
	[Name of Individual] ('the Photographer') [address].
The Photographer has requested permission from the Museum to photograph various items/objects in its collections for the following purposes.	
The Works: Use:	[describe pictures/objects] [name of publication/size/precise use etc.]
Term:	[Proposed period of use]
Territory:	[ ]
Number of Photographs:	[Proposed number of photographs finally to be used]
Dates:	[State proposed dates for shoot]
The Photographs:	The photographs taken or to be taken by the Photographer at the Museum

The Museum has agreed to permit photography for the above purposes on the following terms.

It is agreed as follows:

1. **Liaison**

   The Museum appoints [   ] as its representative in dealing with the Photographer ('the Designated Officer').

2. **Assistance Given**

   The Museum will assist the Photographer so that the Works can be photographed.

3. **Works of Art**

   Paintings must not be moved nor can their glass be removed save with the assistance of the Museum's curatorial staff first approved by the Designated Officer.

4. Compliance by Photographer

The Photographer shall comply with:

- The directions of the Designated Officer and the curatorial and security staff at the Museum

- The Museum's regulations for visitors and the health and safety/fire and other regulations and applicable by-laws and statutes applicable.

5. Assignment

The Photographer hereby assigns to [state exact name of trust/trading company/museum] with full title guarantee by way of present and prospective assignment of copyright and publication right world-wide together with any renewals thereof:

- The copyright in all photographs taken by the Photographer at the Museum whether or not on the Dates

- The copyright in all photographs taken by the Photographer other than at the Museum of the Works and of any paintings, objects or other items in the Museum's collection whether or not on display ('the Objects') and

- All and any publication right arising in respect of the works or the Objects by virtue of their first publication or communication to the public in the form of photographs

6. No consent given to third parties

It is acknowledged and declared that any publication of the Photographs by any third party is and shall be without the consent of the owner of the material depicted in the Photographs whether or not such publication or communication to the public shall be a restricted act within the meaning of the Copyright, Designs & Patents Act 1988.

7. Licence to Photographer

In consideration for the above, the Museum grants the Photographer a non-exclusive licence to publish the Photographs limited to the Use, Term, Territory, and Number of Photographs to be published as set out in the Background above.

8. Credit

The licence is conditional upon the following credit being given to the Museum. '© [   ] Museum 1999'

9. Restriction

The licence granted is personal to the Photographer who may not assign his/her rights as licensee nor may the rights granted by this agreement be assigned, sub-licensed or otherwise transferred to anyone else save with the prior written consent of the Museum.

10. Details of Publication

The Photographer undertakes to supply the Museum with full details of the publication detailed in the Background, its expected date of publication and a [single copy [2 copies]] of the Publication.

11. **Warranty**

The Photographer warrants that all information given to the Museum prior to the date hereof or with regard to the intended use of the Photographs is true and accurate in all respects. The Photographer further warrants that he/she is not taking any Photographs pursuant to any contract of employment.

12. **Indemnity**

The Photographer shall indemnify the Museum against any loss, claim, damage, cost, proceedings or expenses incurred by reason of any breach of this agreement by the Photographer or any act or omission of the Photographer at the Museum or in carrying out the proposed photography.

13. **Third Party Rights**

The Museum does not, generally, own the copyright in any works of art or objects in its collections where copyright subsists. The Photographer acknowledges that it is his/her responsibility, therefore, to secure any relevant copyright permissions from the Design & Artists Copyright Society or the relevant copyright owner as appropriate. The Photographer further undertakes, in relation to the use of any persons depicted in the Photographs, to secure any necessary model releases.

14. **Proper Law**

English law applies.

Signed by _____

[name of the Photographer]

in the presence of _____

AGREEMENT FOR FILMING AT THE MUSEUM

[   ] Museum, address ('the Museum').

[   ] Production Limited [company number (**important – please specify**)] address ('the Film Company').

The Schedule

The Production: [title of film]

Location: [where the filming will take place]

Notification Date: [the date by which the full insurance details need to be with the Museum [see clauses 3 and 19]]

The Dates: [the dates for the shoot]

The Set Up Fee: [the initial fee for the set-up]

The Hourly Fee: [the rate per hour, or part thereof]

The Daily Fee: [the daily rate]

The Filming Regulations: The Regulations Attached

The Credit: [the credit required by the Museum e.g. 'Filmed on location at _____']

IT IS AGREED AS FOLLOWS

1. **Permission for Filming**

   The Museum gives permission, subject to the terms of this agreement and the Filming Regulations, to permit filming at the Location on the Dates for the purpose, only of inclusion of footage in the Production but not otherwise ('the Shoot').

   Any further filming or use of the Location on any other dates other than the Dates shall also be subject to the terms of this agreement and the Filming Regulations.

2. **The Location**

   The location and the objects and collections normally within it, shall remain save for any items which, in the Museum's sole discretion, the Museum wishes to remove and subject to the normal day to day running of the Museum, its exhibition programme and any loans.

3. **Prior Information Required**

   No later than the Notification Date the Film Company shall supply to the Museum a full breakdown of:

   – the equipment that it will be bringing into the Museum

   – the names of all crew (both freelance and employed) who will be assisting at the Shoot either within the Museum or adjacent to it

- the vehicles, trailers and other plant that you will be bringing to the Museum or which will be used outside the Museum in connection with the Shoot

- its requirements in connection with power, water, toilets and other facilities which are to be used

- the proposed location of the vehicles, trailers and plant shown on a sketch plan

- details of any expected difficulties with regard to local traffic, suspension of parking bays and other facilities which might affect the use, enjoyment or access of either the Museum or the surrounding area.

('the Prior Information')

4. **Obligations of Personnel**

The Film Company shall (and shall ensure that its employees, freelances, talent, agents, representatives and persons brought to the Location in connection with the Shoot ('the Personnel') shall) at all times:

- follow promptly and courteously the directions of the Museums' employees regarding access, supplies, parking, movement of vehicles, obstruction and routing of power leads.

- safeguard and keep free from damage or loss the buildings including the walls, skirting boards, flooring, ceiling and other items in and about the fabric of the building as well as the items and objects on display or otherwise at the Location ('the Premises').

- observe any relevant Acts of Parliament, by-laws, regulations, health and safety requirements, fire regulations and other matters affecting the Location or the Shoot in any way

- comply with the Film Regulations

In particular, the Film Company shall ensure that, save with the prior written consent of the Museum, there shall be no:

- smoking

- use of hazardous or flammable chemicals or materials (other than film stock)

at the Location or anywhere within the Museum precincts.

5. **Fees**

The Film Company shall pay:

- the Set Up Fee on the date shown in Schedule I and

- the Daily Fee [or Hourly Fee] in respect of each day [or hours, or part thereof] during which either there is filming at the Location or there remains any plant equipment, personnel or other materials in connection with the Film on the dates shown in Schedule I

- the Facility Fees as detailed in Schedule 2

All fees are exclusive of VAT which shall be added to the fees payable.

The fees have been calculated on the basis that they will be paid on the days stated; if any payments are made late then interest shall be paid thereon at the rate of 5% above the base rate from time to time of Barclays Bank plc (but with a minimum of 12%); interest charges shall be compounded monthly.

6. **Set-Off**

The Film Company shall not be entitled to withhold any payment or make any set-off by reason of there being any dispute between the Museum and the Film Company.

7. **Making Good**

At the conclusion of filming, the Film Company shall make good completely and in all respects any damage to Premises or any part thereof or at the option of the Museum to pay Compensation in relation to the same.

In the event that a work of art or other item within the Museum collections is damaged, lost or destroyed during the Shoot or by reason of any act or default of any of the Personnel, the Film Company shall pay to the Museum its value or, in the case of damage, an amount equivalent to its diminution in value or the cost of restoration, whichever shall be the greater.

8. **Indemnity**

The Film Company shall indemnify and keep the Museum indemnified against all actions, proceedings, costs, claims and demands which may be brought or made against the Museum in respect of personal injury, death or damage to any property whether or not that of the Museum.

9. **Representations**

This permission for filming is given by the Museum based on the representations made by the Film Company including details set out in the Schedule and that the script delivered to the Museum prior to filming is a clear and accurate representation of the nature and narrative of the Film.

10. **Copyright, Model Releases etc.**

The Film Company shall be wholly responsible for any model releases, copyright licences or other permissions which may be necessary to permit any trademark licences to be taken during the Shoot to be used in the Film.

11. **Insurance**

The Film Company shall deliver to the Museum on the Notification Date a certificate of insurance in the name of the Film Company with a respectable insurer sufficient to cover all and any potential liabilities of the Film Company arising or which may arise pursuant to this agreement. This shall be a condition precedent of this agreement and the permission which is being offered by the Museum.

12. **Fitness for Purpose**

It is acknowledged that the Museum is used as a public building for the advancement of education and has not been designed or adapted for the purposes of filming. No warranty is therefore given that the Location or any part of the Museum is safe, appropriate or fit for the purposes of filming and the Film Company shall make its own investigations and satisfy itself that it can carry out the Shoot and comply with its responsibilities under this agreement without jeopardy or danger either to itself, the Personnel or the Museum.

It is declared that the mere delivery of the Prior Information shall not be deemed any acknowledgement or admission that it can comply with the proposal of the Film Company or that the steps taken by the Film Company to comply with the terms of this agreement are appropriate and reasonable.

13. **The Film**

Within 21 days of the date hereof or the Notification Date whichever is the earlier the Film Company shall give the Museum a synopsis of the script and, additionally, extracts from the script of those scenes which are to be filmed at the Location together with such further information regarding the terms and scope of the film as the Museum may request ('the Outline Story').

14. **Credit**

The Film Company shall insert the Credit on all copies of the Film and ensure that the Credit is shown as part of the Film whether on theatrical release, video or other usage. Any other reference to the Museum or the Location shall be in a form agreed by the Museum in advance, in writing.

15. **Editorial Control**

It is accepted that the editorial decision of the Film Company in respect of the footage used is final unless the material to be shot varies materially from that included in the synopsis and extracts from the script delivered to the Museum under 13 above.

16. **Termination**

Either party may terminate this Agreement forthwith if:

● The other party is in material or persistent breach of any of these terms and a period of 14 days has elapsed since the party wishing to terminate has notified the other of the breach and the other party has failed to remedy the same.

The Museum may terminate this Agreement by notice in writing to the Film Company if:

● Any of the Personnel shall be guilty of gross misconduct

● The scenes being shot at the Location differ materially from those outlined in the Outline Story

● Damage or loss occurs to any of the Premises during the period that any of the Personnel are at the Location.

17. **Effect of Termination**

On termination, the permission given in clause 1 ceases with immediate effect.

Termination of this Agreement howsoever caused shall not affect:

● The rights and obligations of both parties under this Agreement in the period up to the date of termination;

● The rights and obligations of both parties under this Agreement which by their nature are due to continue beyond such termination and/or

● The rights of the Museum to recover any monies payable pursuant to clause 5 or otherwise above

On termination, the Museum shall be under no obligation to refund or return any payments made to them by the Film Company.

18. **No Assignment**

The Film Company shall not be entitled to assign this Agreement or sub-license or transfer any of its rights and obligations hereunder save (a) to a completion guarantor notified to the Museum by the Notification Date or (b) with prior written consent of the Museum.

19. **General**

All notices (excluding routine communications) to be served by one party on the other shall be deemed duly delivered or served:

- Within two days of posting if posted by first class pre-paid post to the address of the other party stated above or such other address as may be notified in accordance herewith or

- Immediately on delivery by hand to such address or

- In the case of service on the Film Company by delivery of notice by hand to any of the director, the assistant director or an executive producer at the Location

No failure or delay on the part of the Museum to exercise any right, power, remedy or privilege hereunder shall operate as a waiver thereof.

This agreement shall supersede all other arrangements or agreements (whether oral or in writing) between the parties as to this subject matter and, in the event of any inconsistency between this Agreement and any terms and conditions put forward by the Film Company the terms of this Agreement shall, unless otherwise specifically agreed in writing by the Museum, prevail.

No variation of this Agreement shall be made unless in writing and agreed by both parties.

Nothing in this Agreement shall be construed as making the Museum and the Film Company partners nor in the position of principal or agent of each other; neither party shall be able to bind the other in any way.

Each party shall be responsible for its own costs (if any) incurred in relation to the preparation and execution of this Agreement.

20. **Definitions**

The words stated have the meanings stated alongside in the Schedule which is incorporated into this Agreement.

21. **Governing Law**

This Agreement is to be governed by and construed in accordance with the laws of England and the parties submit to the jurisdiction of the High Court of England and Wales.

(*A Guide to Copyright for Museums and Galleries*, Routledge: 2000)

SCHEDULE 1

Set Up Fee: To be paid on [   ]

The Hourly Fees: To be paid on [   ]

The Daily Fees: To be paid on [   ]

SCHEDULE 2

The Facility Fees namely [detail assistance and costs involved]

To be paid on [   ]

FILMING REGULATIONS

[These can include administrative/practical/technical matters etc.]

- Security arrangements
- Contact names
- Light levels permissible
- Methods of attaching cables/tracking
- Catering/toilet facilities

Signed _____

for and on behalf of _____ [The Trustees of the Museum]

Signed by _____

for and on behalf of _____ [The Film Company]

(A Guide to Copyright for Museums and Galleries, Routledge: 2000)

BOOK PUBLISHING AGREEMENT

Date:

Parties:

(1) [Name of museum/gallery legal entity] of [insert address] ('the Publisher') and

(2) [Name of author] of [insert address] ('the Author')

WHEREAS:

(A) The Author is the author of copyright in the Work (as defined below) and wishes to publish the Work

(B) The Publisher has agreed to publish the Work subject to the terms set out below

IT IS HEREBY AGREED between the parties that:

1. **Definitions and Interpretation**

   1.1   In this Agreement and its Schedules the following words have the following meanings:

'the Advance'	means the sum of money set out in Schedule 2;
'Delivery Date'	means the date for delivery of the Author's typescripts of the Work as set out in Schedule 3;
'Desired Length'	means the minimum number of words to be contained in the Author's typescript of the Work as set out in Schedule 4;
'the Format'	means the computer disk format set out in Schedule 5;
'Illustrations'	means and includes without limitation photographs, pictures, diagrams, drawings, maps, tables, charts and graphs;
'the Language'	means the language(s) set out in Schedule 6;
'the Outline'	means any outline or commission given by the Publisher to the Author or the Author in relation to the preparation of the Work;
'the Royalties'	means the percentages as set out in Part 1 of Schedule 7;
'the Term'	means the period set out in Schedule 1
'Territory'	means the countries or geographical areas listed in Schedule 8;
'the Work'	means the work the title of which is set out in Schedule 9 including any Illustrations and index created by the Author; and

'Volume Form'	means and includes without limitation all forms of publication whether hardback, paperback, book club, anthology, abridgement, condensation, digest or selection (whether of textual, graphic or other materials), computer program, compact disc, digital/analogue, 'on-line' communication or any other means of reproducing or displaying the Work or parts of it which are now known or which become known, including reproduction by sound or audio-visual recording.

1.2 The headings used in this Agreement are included for convenience only and are not to be used in construing or interpreting this Agreement.

1.3 In this Agreement:

(a) any reference to the plural shall include the singular and any reference to the singular shall include the plural; and

(b) any reference to a Clause or a Schedule shall be to a clause or a schedule of this Agreement.

2. Grants of Rights

2.1 The Author hereby grants to the Publisher the following rights:

(a) the exclusive right and licence to produce, publish, distribute, rent and sell the Work or any abridgement in Volume Form (including parts or extracts and whether with or without material by other authors) in the Languages for the Term; and

(b) the exclusive right to further license the above-mentioned rights to others.

2.2 The Author further and in addition to any rights already granted above, appoints the Publisher as its exclusive agent in respect of all rights in Part 2 of Schedule 7.

2.3 The Author hereby waives any moral rights pursuant to section 80 of the Copyright, Designs and Patents Act 1988 or any similar or analogous right in any area of the Territory.[1]

3. Term

This Agreement shall commence on the date hereof and shall continue, subject to the provisions of Clause 14 for the Term.

4. Author's General Obligations

4.1 The Author shall arrange for two copies of the complete typescript of the Work including Illustrations but excluding any index to be delivered to the Publishers by no later than close of business on the Delivery Date, time being of the essence. The Author shall retain at least one duplicate of the typescript of the Work.

---

[1] This does not waive the Author's moral rights to be identified as the Author. It does however waive the Author's right to object to certain forms of editing the work.

(*A Guide to Copyright for Museums and Galleries*, Routledge: 2000)

4.2 The typescript copies shall be clearly typed using double spacing on single sides of A4 paper and be of the Desired Length plus or minus five percent (5%). A margin of at least 1 inch (2.5cm) should border the page.

4.3 Authorship in the physical property of the typescript copies delivered to the Publisher shall pass to the Publisher upon delivery.

4.4 Unless otherwise expressly agreed in writing the Author shall also deliver a copy of the Work on computer disk in the Format.

4.5 The Work delivered shall be in all other respects acceptable to the Publisher and in particular:

(a) shall be prepared with all due care; and

(b) shall conform to any Outline.

4.6 Should the above-mentioned obligations in this clause not be met by the Delivery Date, the Publisher may at its option extend the Delivery Date by notice in writing (time remaining of the essence) or may by notice in writing terminate this Agreement.

4.7 Where the Agreement is terminated by the Publisher pursuant to this clause the Author shall immediately repay to the Publisher any Advance and any other monies to the Publisher paid to the Author in connection with the Work.

4.8 The Author shall not for the duration of this Agreement without the consent in writing of the Publisher offer for publication otherwise than to the Publisher any work of a nature which may reasonably be considered by the Publisher to be likely to affect prejudicially the sales of the Work.

4.9 Without prejudice to its other rights under this Agreement, in the event that the Author does not meet the Author's obligations under this clause the Publisher shall be entitled to reduce any instalments of the Advance due by 25% of the total instalment due for every 30 day period which passes after the due date of performance of the relevant obligation in this clause before the Author performs such obligation.

5. **Publisher's General Obligations**

5.1 The Publisher shall publish the Work at its own expense subject to the Author complying in full with the terms and conditions of the Agreement.

5.2 The Publisher shall pay the Advance to the Author on account of all monies due to the Author under this Agreement. The Advance shall be payable to the Author as set out in Schedule 2 and shall be set against and deducted from the Royalties due under this clause.

5.3 The Publisher shall pay to the Author the Royalties on net amounts actually received by the Publisher in respect of exploitation of the rights set out in Part 1 of Schedule 7.[2] In respect of the rights set out in Part

---

[2] Where the Publisher is actually producing and selling product, it is normal to pay a percentage of net receipts – here, Part 1 of the Schedule. Where the Publisher sub-licenses to others, or acts as agent for the sale or licence of rights, a percentage of the fees received are paid back to the Author – here, Part 2 of the Schedule.

2 of Schedule 7 the Publisher shall pay to the Author the percentages of all fees, advances and royalties received by the Publisher as set out in Schedule 7 in respect of such rights.

5.4 The Royalties shall be reduced by mutual agreement if in order to keep the Work in print the Publisher proposes to issue a small reprinting which due to economies of scale would be unprofitable to print at the current Royalties.

5.5 The Publisher shall send to the Author on the day of first publication of the Work [number] free copies of the published Work. The Author shall be entitled to purchase further copies for personal use on the Publisher's usual terms but shall not be entitled to resell, rent or otherwise distribute such copies.

6. Illustrations and Permissions

6.1 If in the opinion of the Publisher and the Author any Illustrations are desirable for inclusion in the Work then the full nature and extent of such Illustrations shall be agreed by the parties.

6.2 Unless otherwise expressly agreed in writing the Author shall obtain free of charge for the Publisher's use copies of agreed Illustrations. Authorship of the physical property in such copies of the agreed Illustrations shall pass to the Publisher upon delivery.

6.3 If a Work contains any Illustrations or other material, copyright in which is not vested in the Author, the Author shall obtain free of charge for the Publisher written permission from the appropriate copyright Author for the Publisher's use of any such material in any edition of the Work pursuant to this Agreement, including editions or versions licensed by the Publisher to the others. The Author shall pay any fee required by the grantor of such permission and shall upon request from the Publisher deliver to the Publisher copies of any permission so obtained and proof of payment of any fee for such permission.

7. Index

If in the opinion of the Publisher the Work requires an index, the Author shall supply a suitable index at the time that page proofs are corrected for press. Should the Author be unable or decline to supply such an index or indicate an intention not to supply such an index when required, the Publisher may arrange for the preparation of the index and shall be entitled to charge costs of preparation to the Author.

8. Proofs and Alterations

The Author shall read, check and correct proofs of the Work and shall return them to the Publisher with any necessary corrections within fourteen days of their receipt, failing which the Publisher may consider the proofs as passed for press. The cost of the Author's alterations to proofs (other than the correction of typesetter's errors) including finished Illustrations and indexes, which are in excess of five per cent (5%) of the length of the Work, shall be paid for by the Author.

9. Production, Advertising and Selling

The Publisher shall have entire control over the production of the Work, the paper, printing, binding, jacket and embellishments for the Work, the manner and extent of advertisement, the title under which the Work is published, any other material to be published with the Work and the number and distribution of free copies to the press and otherwise. The Publisher shall also have control over the price, format and terms of sale of the first and any subsequent editions of the Work. Except as otherwise specified the Publisher shall be responsible for the entire cost of producing, advertising and selling the Work.

10. Accounts

10.1 The Publisher shall make up accounts relating to exploitation of Work to 31 March or 30 September (whichever occurs sooner) following the date of first publication of the Work by the Publisher, and subsequently twice annually to 31 March and 30 September. Subject to Clause 10.2 below these accounts shall be sent to the Author during the next succeeding months of July and January respectively, together with any payment due to the Author.

10.2 No payment need be made by the Publisher in respect of any period in which the sum due to the Author is less than fifty pounds (£50), in which case such sum will be carried forward to the next accounting date.

10.3 The Publisher shall be entitled at the first accounting after publication or reissue of the Work to deduct from payments due to the Author a sum representing a reserve against return. This reserve sum shall, to the extent not utilised by the Publisher, be credited to the Author's account at the fourth accounting after publication or reissue of the Work. The sum so deducted shall be calculated as set out in Schedule 10. Where in the Publisher's sole opinion it is necessary in the light of more recent returns experience to alter the amounts of such sum, Schedule 10 may be revised accordingly provided that under no circumstances shall the reserve sum exceed twenty per cent (20%) of the Publisher's net receipts.

10.4 The Publisher shall be entitled to deduct from any amounts due to the Author any sums owed to the Publisher by the Author pursuant to this Agreement.

10.5 The Author may at their own expense audit the Publisher's books of account relating to exploitation of the Work at the place where such books are kept in order to verify the Royalties statements in respect of the Work. Any such audit shall be conducted by an independent professional auditor during business hours and in such a manner as not to interfere with the Publisher's normal business activities. A copy of any report made by such auditor shall be delivered to the Publisher at the same time as the report is delivered to the Author. No audit in respect of any Royalties statement shall commence later than twenty-four (24) months from the date of such statement and only one audit shall be conducted in respect of any such statement.

11. **Remainders**

Should the Publisher at any time consider it necessary to dispose of all the remaining copies of the Work as a remainder, it shall offer to the Author four weeks' option to purchase such copies at the remainder price. No Royalties shall be paid on copies sold to the Author under this provision.

12. **Option**

12.1 The Author agrees to give the Publisher the right of first refusal (including the first opportunity to read and consider for publication) to the Author's next non-fiction work suitable for publication. The Author shall offer to the Publisher the same rights and Territory granted to the Publisher in this Agreement. Such work shall be the subject of a fresh agreement on terms which shall be fair and reasonable. If the parties are unable to reach agreement with respect to the terms of publishing the new work within the time limits indicated in this Option clause, then the Author shall be free to offer the same to others, but only upon terms which are more favourable to the Author than those offered by the Publisher.

12.2 The Publisher shall notify the Author of its acceptance or otherwise of terms in writing within [six (6) weeks] of receipt of the offer by the Author, provided that the Publisher shall not be required to exercise any option until [(6) months] after publication of the Work.

13. **Warranty, Indemnity and Insurance**

13.1 The Author warrants and undertakes to the Publisher that:

(a) the Author is entitled to enter into this Agreement and to grant the rights and licences given to the Publisher;

(b) the Work does not infringe or violate any legal or moral rights belonging to any other party and that any fee royalties or commission due to any person, firm or company having any interest in the Work or in any material included in the Work has been or shall be paid in time by the Author;

(c) all statements contained in the Work purporting to be facts are true and accurate;

(d) the Work contains nothing objectionable, libellous, obscene, improper, scandalous, indecent, blasphemous or which is a breach of the Official Secrets Act or which is in any way unlawful;

(e) the Work contains no statement, information, advice, instruction, recipe or formula which, if acted upon by a user or reader, could cause physical injury, damage or financial loss; and

(f) the Work is not and has not been the subject of any complaint, claim or legal proceedings.

13.2 The Author agrees to indemnify the Publisher and hold it harmless against and pay on behalf of or reimburse it in respect of any claim, loss, liability, damage or expense (including legal costs and expenses) which the Publisher may suffer, sustain or become subject to as a result of any breach by the Author of:

(a) the conditions contained in this clause; and

(b) the condition in Clause 6.3 above.

13.3 Should the Publisher or its legal advisors consider that any material contained in the Work may be considered objectionable or likely to be actionable at law, the Publisher may request the Author to alter or amend the Work in such a way as may appear appropriate. Any such alterations or amendments shall be without prejudice to and shall not affect the Author's liability under the Author's warranties and indemnity contained in this Agreement. Should the Author refuse to alter or amend the Work in accordance with the Publisher's request, the Author shall at once repay to the Publisher any monies already paid by the Publisher to the Author (including the Advance) in connection with the Work and this Agreement shall (without prejudice to any other rights the Publisher may have) immediately terminate.

13.4 If in the opinion of the Publisher it is necessary to have the Work read for libellous or other unlawful material, the cost of such reading shall be borne by the Author.

14. Copyright Infringement

14.1 If at any time during the term of this Agreement the copyright of the Work in the reasonable opinion of the Publishers is infringed, and the Author after receiving written notice of such infringement from the Publisher refuses or neglects to take proceedings in respect of the infringement on behalf of the Publisher, the Publisher shall be entitled to take proceedings in the joint names of the Publisher and the Author upon giving the Author a sufficient and reasonable security to indemnify the Author against any liability for costs. The Author shall provide all reasonable assistance required by the Publisher and shall co-operate with the Publisher. In this event, any sum received by way of damages shall belong to the Publisher.

14.2 The provisions of the clause are intended to apply only in the case of an infringement in the copyright of the Work affecting the interests granted to the Publisher under this Agreement.

15. Termination

15.1 If at any time the Publisher allows the Work to go out of print or off the market in all editions issued by the Publisher or authorised by it, as the Publisher shall be entitled to do in its sole discretion, and if within six (6) months of having received a written request from the Author to do so, the Publisher has not reprinted and placed on the market a new edition or authorised the same then all rights granted under this Agreement shall immediately and without further notice revert to the Author (except those deriving from the option in Clause 12) without prejudice to all rights of the Publisher in respect of any contracts or negotiations properly entered into by it with any third party prior to the date of such reversion, and without prejudice to any monies already paid or due to the Author from the Publisher.

15.2 Should the Publisher at any time itself or through anyone acting on its behalf fail to comply with any of the clauses or conditions set out in this Agreement within two (2) months after written notice from the Author to rectify such failure, or should the Publisher go into liquidation (other than voluntary liquidation for the purpose of reconstruction) then in either event all rights granted under this Agreement shall revert to the Author forthwith and without further notice, without prejudice to all rights of the Publisher in respect of any contracts or negotiations properly entered into by it and any third party prior to the date of such reversion, and without prejudice to any monies already paid or then due to the Author from the Publisher.

15.3 Upon termination of this Agreement by the Author for whatever reason, the Publisher shall be entitled for a period of twelve months from such termination to sell remaining stocks of the Work in its possession or control as at the date of termination subject always to payment of the Royalties in accordance with the provisions of this Agreement.

15.4 Should the Author fail to comply with any of the clauses or conditions set out in this Agreement and fail to rectify such failure within 30 days after written notice from the Publisher, the Publisher shall without prejudice to any other rights or remedies it may have be entitled to terminate the contract without further notice.

16. **Assignment**

The Publisher shall be entitled to assign all of its rights and obligations acquired pursuant to this Agreement.

17. **Severability**

In the event that any one or more of these terms shall be held to be invalid, illegal or unenforceable in any respect the validity, legality and enforceability of the remaining provisions shall not in any way be affected.

18. **Waiver**

Failure on the part of either party to exercise or enforce any rights conferred in these terms shall not be deemed to be a waiver of any such right nor operate so as to bar the exercise or enforcement of such right at any other time.

19. **Governing Law**

The construction, validity and performance of this Agreement shall be governed, construed and interpreted in accordance with the laws in England, and the parties agree to submit to the non-exclusive jurisdiction of the courts of England and Wales.

SCHEDULES

SCHEDULE 1

Term[3]: The term shall be [   ] years from the date of this Agreement/the legal term of copyright throughout the Territory

SCHEDULE 2

Advance Payment: (i) Amount:

  (ii) The payment shall be made as follows:

(a) [   ] £ on signature

(b) [   ] £ on delivery and acceptance

SCHEDULE 3

Delivery Date:

SCHEDULE 4

Desired Length: [number of words]

SCHEDULE 5

Format: Disks supplied must:

(i)   allow for an exact reproduction of the typescript referred to in Clauses 4.1 and 4.2 of this Agreement

(ii) be supplied in [insert acceptable word processing packages]

(iii) be 3½″ double sided, double density 3

SCHEDULE 6

Languages: English

SCHEDULE 7

Part 1

(a) copies of books sold in Britain, Northern Ireland, Irish Republic, Isle of Man, Channel Islands ('Home Market')

(i) hardback   :   [   ]% [of published UK price]/[of Publisher's net receipts]

(ii) paperback   :   [   ]% [of published UK price]/[of Publisher's net receipts]

[3] It is common for Publishers to take licences for the full term of copyright. Where the licence is exclusive, this is arguably 'anti-competitive' and shorter terms should be considered.

(b) copies of books sold for export or at discounts of more than 50%:

[   ]% of Publisher's net receipts

(c) low priced, hardcover reprints: [   ]% of Publisher's net receipts

Part 2

(a) serialisation/extracts/abridgements in periodicals	[	]%
(b) dramatisation, musical, documentary rights in any medium	[	]%
(c) US rights	[	]%
(d) translation rights	[	]%
(e) radio and television straight recording rights	[	]%
(f) mechanical rights (records, tapes)	[	]%
(g) merchandising rights	[	]%
(h) strip cartoons or picturisation rights	[	]%
(i) electronic publishing rights	[	]%
(j) anthology rights	[	]%
(k) digest, one-shot syndication, condensation rights	[	]%
(l) talking books	[	]%
(m) educational, hardcover reprint rights, book club, large print editions	[	]%
(n) paperback rights licensed to another publisher	[	]%
(o) microphotographic and xerographic rights (including participation in the Copyright Licensing Agency licensing scheme)	[	]%

SCHEDULE 8

Territory: [Worldwide]

SCHEDULE 9

The Work (Title):

SCHEDULE 10

Reserve Against Returns:

IN WITNESS whereof the parties have signed this Agreement on the date appearing at the head of the Agreement

SIGNED by _____

for and on behalf of [the Publisher]

Signed by _____ [the Author]

MERCHANDISING AGREEMENT

Date:

Parties:

1. [Name of Licensor, address] ('the Museum') which expression shall include its successors in title and assigns.

2. [Name of Licensee, address] ('The Licensee').

The parties agree as follows:

1. **Interpretation**

   1.1 In this Agreement the following expressions shall have the following meanings:

'Associate'	means the Licensee itself but also includes any subsidiary of the Licensee or any other person, firm or corporation associated in any manner with the Licensee or its officers, directors or major shareholders;
'Guaranteed Payment'	means that sum set forth in Part III of Schedule E;
'Initial Payment'	means that sum set forth in Part I of Schedule E;
'Licence'	means the licence granted to the Licensee by the Museum pursuant to clause 2;
'Licence Term'	means the term from the date of this Agreement up to the date set forth in Schedule D hereof;
'Licensed Products'	means those products set forth in Schedule B hereof;
'Net Sales'	means the gross point of sale price or value of the Licensed Products actually charged by the Licensee or others to retail stores and bona fide wholesalers less any value added tax or sales tax, quantity discounts, usual trade discounts to customers and refunds for returns, but not including any deductions for cash or other discounts or agency commission;
'Property'	[describe copyright and/or intellectual property to be licensed by the Licensor] as more particularly described in Schedule A hereof;
'Territory'	means that country [those countries] set forth in Schedule C hereof.

   1.2 References to Clauses and Schedules are to clauses of and schedules to this Agreement.

   1.3 Unless the context otherwise requires, words importing the singular only shall include the plural and vice versa, words importing any gender shall include all other genders and words importing natural persons shall include corporations.

1.4 Headings to Clauses and Schedules are for convenience only and do not affect the interpretation of this Agreement.

1.5 The Schedules form part of this Agreement and shall have the same force and effect as if expressly set out in the body of this Agreement, and any reference to this Agreement shall include the Schedules.

2. **Licence**

2.1 The Museum hereby grants to the Licensee for the Licence Term subject to the terms and conditions hereinafter contained a licence in the Territory to use the Property solely in connection with the manufacture, distribution and sale of the Licensed Products.

2.2 The Licensee shall be in respect of the Territory. The Licensee will not actively solicit purchasers of the Licensed Product(s) outside the Territory.

2.3 The Licence shall continue for the Licence Term unless sooner terminated in accordance with the terms and conditions hereof.

3. **Consideration**

3.1 In consideration of the grant of the Licence the Licensee agrees to pay to the Museum:

3.1.1 upon signature hereof the Initial Payment which shall subject to the terms of the proviso to sub-clause 3.2 hereof stand to the credit of the Licence Fee;

3.1.2 upon the dates set out in clause 4 hereof during the Licence Term (with each statement referred to in clause 4 hereof) the Licence Fee in respect of all net sales of the Licensed Products by the Licensee or any Associate, its agents, licensees or distributors (and which shall include all the Licensed Products distributed by the Licensee or others as aforesaid).

3.2 The Licensee guarantees to the Museum that an amount equal to the Guaranteed Payment shall have been paid to the Museum in respect of the Licence Fee at the expiration of the Licence Term or earlier termination (but excluding any payment made in respect of the Initial Payment). If the Museum shall at the expiration of the Licence Term have received less than the Guaranteed Payment sum then the Museum shall require the Licensee to pay and the Licensee shall pay to the Museum immediately upon demand the difference between the Guaranteed Payment and the sums actually received by the Museum (other than the Initial Payment) during the Licence Term PROVIDED THAT in no event shall any part of the Initial Payment, the Guaranteed Payment or the Licence Fee received by the Museum be repayable by it to the Licensee.

3.3 Time shall be of the essence in respect of any or all of the Licensee's obligations to make payment hereunder or to commence manufacture or distribution of any of the Products.

3.4 In the event that the Licensee shall fail to make any payment hereunder by the due date interest shall be charged upon the outstanding amount by the Museum at a rate of 2.5 per cent per annum above the Base Rate from time to time charged by [insert name of Museum bank] Bank Plc from the due date until such date as payment of that amount is made and received by the Museum.

3.5 All payments to be made by the Licensee to the Museum hereunder shall be exclusive of Value Added Tax which shall be paid by the Museum (where applicable) upon submission of the appropriate Value Added Tax invoice.

4. **Statements of Account and Payment of Fees**

4.1 The Licensee shall within fifteen days after the period ending respectively 31 March, 30 June, 30 September and 31 December in any calendar year during the Licence Term furnish to the Museum a complete and accurate statement for each Licensed Product(s) and in respect of each country comprising the Territory in respect of such period showing the number, description and gross sale price or value itemised deductions from the gross sale price or value and net sales of each of the Licensed Product(s) distributed and/or sold by the Licensee during the Term last ended to which the statements refer. The statements shall be furnished to the Museum as aforesaid whether or not any of the Licensed Product(s) have been sold during such Term and shall be certified to be accurate by an officer of the Licensee. Receipt or acceptance by the Museum of any of the statements furnished pursuant to this Licence or of any sums paid hereunder shall not preclude the Museum from questioning the correctness thereof at any time and in the event that any inconsistencies or mistakes in payments are discovered in such statements they shall immediately be rectified and the appropriate payments made by the Licensee.

4.2 Simultaneously with the sending of each statement referred to in the preceding clause the Licensee shall pay to the Museum the appropriate Licence Fee covered by the statement.

5. **Accounting Records and Rights of Inspection**

5.1 The Licensee shall keep accurate books of account and records covering all transactions relating to this Licence and the duly authorised representatives of the Museum shall have the right on two business days' notice in writing at a reasonable hour of the day to an examination of the said books of account and records and of all other documents and material in the possession or under the control of the Licensee with respect to the subject matter and the terms of this Licence and shall have free and full access thereto for said purposes and for the purpose of making extracts therefrom. The Museum agrees that it will conduct no more than two examinations pursuant to the terms of this clause during any twelve month period of the Licence Term. The Licensee shall make available all such books of account and records for at least six years after the termination of the Licence Term (or any extended period) and the Licensee agrees to permit inspection thereof by the Museum during such six year Term.

6. Trade Marks

6.1 The Museum will take such steps as it considers reasonable (having regard to costs and risk) to obtain trademark registration in respect of the Property covering the Licensed Product(s) in relevant parts of the Territory and together with the Licensee will use its best endeavours to secure the registration of the Licensee as registered user of any such registered trade marks upon such terms consistent with the terms of this Licence as may be acceptable to the relevant Registrar of Trade Marks. The Licensee hereby agrees and undertakes to sign and complete all such documents which may be required to be signed by it for the purpose of such registration and in default of such signature, hereby appoints the Museum's authorised representatives as its duly authorised attorney for such purpose. The Museum gives no warranty that any of the above registrations will be granted and the refusal of any such registrations will in no way affect the obligations of the Licensee hereunder. The costs of such registrations (including registration of licences) shall be borne by the Museum and the Licensee in equal shares.

7. Licensee's Covenants

7.1 The Licensee covenants with the Museum that:

7.1.1 each and every one of the Licensed Product(s) including the packaging, labels, containers, advertisements and/or related material shall contain such copyright and/or trade mark and/or such other relevant notices as shall be required and/or approved by the Museum;

7.1.2 it will indemnify the Museum and undertakes to defend the Museum against and hold it harmless from all claims, actions, loss or liability (including reasonable legal fees incurred) arising out of any alleged unauthorised use of any patent, process, copyright, trade mark (other than the Museum's trade mark), idea, method or device by the Licensee in connection with the Licensed Product(s) and also from any claims, action, loss or liability (including reasonable legal fees incurred) arising out of or based upon alleged defects in such Products;

7.1.3 it will obtain and maintain during the Licence Term at its own expense product liability insurance for both the Museum and itself from a well-recognised Museum insurer, providing coverage at least in the amount of £   for each claim and in the aggregate or the local currency of the Territory equivalent against any legal fees incurred arising out of or based upon alleged defects in the Licensed Products. The Licensee will provide the Museum with a certificate evidencing such insurance prior to the sale of any Licensed Products, and arrange for a note of the Museum's interest to be endorsed on the policy;

7.1.4 it will not make any representation or give any warranty on behalf of the Museum;

7.1.5 it will not at any time do or suffer to be done any act or thing which will in any way impair or affect the Property or the rights and interests of the Museum therein;

(A Guide to Copyright for Museums and Galleries, Routledge: 2000)

7.1.6 it will at its own expense procure and maintain insurance in respect of the materials supplied to the Museum pursuant to this Agreement whilst the same are in transit or remain in the possession or control of the Museum and it acknowledges that the Museum shall have no liability whatsoever for any loss or damage to such materials at any time;

7.1.7 it will procure that the Licensed Product(s) comply with all the safety standards or codes applicable in the Territory to the manufacture of goods of the nature of the Licensed Product(s) and will furnish the Museum as soon as possible with evidence satisfactory to the Museum of such compliance.

8. Museum's Warranty

8.1 The Museum hereby agrees and warrants to the Licensee that it is the owner of all rights needed for the exploitation by the Licensee of its rights hereunder and the Museum has good title and full authority to enter into this Agreement and to give and enter into the warranties, covenants and agreements herein contained. In the event of any third party infringing or attempting to infringe during the Licence Term any rights acquired by the Licensee hereunder the Licensee shall inform the Museum immediately of such infringement or attempted infringement. In the event that the Museum decides within its absolute discretion that proceedings shall be commenced the Licensee shall provide all information and assistance to the Museum that may be necessary. The Museum shall bear the costs of any such proceedings but shall be entitled to retain all damages covered.

9. Approvals

9.1 The Licensee agrees to obtain the written approval of the Museum concerning all aspect of the design of the Licensed Product(s) including but without limitation the packaging of the Product(s), the material of manufacture, samples of the designs for each of the Licensed Product(s) and all 'point of sale materials', which approval shall be given or withheld at the absolute discretion of the Museum. None of the Product(s) shall be distributed or sold by the Licensee without such prior written approval.

9.2 The Licensee shall ensure or procure that the Licensed Product(s) together with all the aforesaid wrappings, containers, contents, display materials and the like shall conform with the samples approved by the Museum.

10. Restrictions upon the Licensee

10.1 The Licensee shall only sell the Licensed Product(s) either to bona fide independent wholesalers (which are not Associates) or retailers for resale and distribution directly to the public, in all cases in the course of normal cash trading and in particular (but not by way of limitation) shall not sell or distribute the Product(s) to hawkers, peddlers, or street vendors. Should the Licensee wish to undertake distribution and sale of the Licensed Product(s) by any method or means not hereby authorised the Licensee shall notify the Museum in writing accordingly and shall furnish the Museum with particulars of the Licensee's proposals concerning such distribution and sale to which the Museum may give or withhold its consent in its absolute discretion.

10.2 If the Licensee sells or distributes any of the Licensed Product(s) at a special price or for no consideration directly or indirectly to any of its Associates the Licensee shall nevertheless (without prejudice to the rights and remedies of the Museum in respect of such unauthorised sale or distribution) pay the Licence Fee with respect to such sales or distribution based upon the price generally charged to the trade by the Licensee or by its Associates.

11. **Prohibitions upon the Licensee**

11.1 During the Licence Term and any extension thereof and thereafter the Licensee agrees that:

11.1.1 it will not alter, harm, misuse or bring into disrepute the Property in any way whatsoever;

11.1.2 All expenses attributable to the design and manufacture of the Licensed Product(s) shall be borne by it alone;

11.1.3 it will not enter into any sub-licence or agency agreement for the manufacture, sale or distribution of the Licensed Product(s) without the prior written consent of the Museum which the Museum may give or withhold in its absolute discretion PROVIDED THAT the Licensee shall be entitled to contract a third party to manufacture the Licensed Product(s) if and only if:

11.1.3.1 the Museum approves in writing the identity of such third party manufacturer; and

11.1.3.2 the Licensee procures the execution of an agreement with the manufacturer in such form as the Museum may require or approve governing the use of the Property; and

11.1.3.3 it will not enter into any agreement relating to the Property for commercial tie-ups or promotions with any third party without the prior written consent of the Museum which the Museum may give or withhold in its absolute discretion.

12. **Events of Termination**

12.1 If the Licensee does not commence in good faith to manufacture and distribute and sell each of the Licensed Product(s) in quantities which are appropriate for first run sales of goods similar to the Licensed Product(s) in the Territory on or before the dates specified in Schedule F hereof the Museum in addition to all other remedies available to it shall have at any time after such dates as aforesaid (without prejudice to any remedy in respect of any prior default of the Licensee) the option to terminate the Licence granted hereunder forthwith with respect to such of the Licensed Product(s) upon giving to the Licensee notice of such termination.

12.2 This Agreement may be terminated:

12.2.1 forthwith by either party on giving notice in writing to the other if the other commits any material breach of any term of this

Agreement and which (in the case of a breach capable of being remedied) shall not have been remedied within 30 Business Days of a written request to remedy the same (such request to contain a warning of the intention to terminate); or

12.2.2 forthwith by either party on giving notice in writing to the other if the other shall convene a meeting of its creditors or if a proposal shall be made for a voluntary arrangement within Part 1 of the UK Insolvency Act 1986 or a proposal for any other composition scheme or arrangement with (or assignment for the benefit of) its debts within the meaning of Section 123 of the UK Insolvency Act 1986 or if a trustee receiver, or administrative receiver or similar officer is appointed in respect of all or any part of the business or assets of the other party or if a petition is presented or a meeting is convened for the purpose of considering a resolution or other steps are taken for the winding-up of the other party or for the making of an administration order (otherwise than for the purpose of a solvent amalgamation or reconstruction) or if any analogous event to any of these listed herein occurs in any part of the Territory; or

12.2.3 by the Museum in the event that there is a change in the identity of the owner of the controlling interest in the Licensee (and for this purpose, 'controlling interest' means either:

(i) the ownership or control (directly or indirectly) of more than 50% of the Licensee's voting share capital or the share capital of the Licensee's holding company; or

(ii) the ability to direct the casting of more than 50% of the votes exercisable at general meetings or those of the Licensee's holding company on all, or substantially all, matters).

12.3 Any termination of this Agreement shall be without prejudice to any rights or remedies a party may be entitled to hereunder or at law and shall not affect any accrued rights or liabilities of either party, nor the coming into or continuance in force of any provision hereof which is expressly or by implication intended to come into or continue in force on or after such termination.

12.4 On the termination for any cause whatsoever of the Licence granted hereunder all fees accrued shall become immediately due and payable to the Museum and the Museum shall not be obliged to reimburse the Licensee for any Initial Payment or Guaranteed Payment already paid by the Licensee and the Licensee shall at no time and under no circumstances be entitled to recover payment of any Licence Fee or part thereof paid to the Museum.

13. **Term of sell-off**

13.1 On expiry of the Licence Term by effluxion of time the Licensee shall (subject as hereinafter provided) nevertheless have the right to sell off or cause to be sold off the balance of the Licensed Product(s) already manufactured or in the process of manufacture at the time of such expiry but in no event shall such right extend beyond a Term of three calendar months from the date of such termination. The obligations of the Licensee to make the payments herein provided shall also continue and remain in force and effect. On expiry of the Term of sell-off the Licensee shall immediately destroy or procure the destruction of the balance of the Licensed Product(s) then remaining in stock and shall furnish to the Museum a certificate in a form acceptable to the Museum evidencing such destruction and signed by an officer of the Museum or by an independent third party as the Museum may require. The right of sell-off granted to the Licensee hereunder shall not apply in the event that this Licence is terminated by the Museum prior to its expiry by effluxion of time.

14. **Licensee's Obligations upon Termination**

14.1 On the termination of this Licence for whatever reason the Licensee shall delivery forthwith to the Museum a statement indicating the number and description of the Licensed Product(s) in stock or in process of manufacture as at (a) sixty days prior to the expiration of this Licence and (b) fifteen days after receipt from the Museum of a notice terminating this Licence or if no such notice is required fifteen days after the occurrence of any event which terminates this Licence.

14.2 If for any reason the Licensee shall not be entitled on termination of this Licence to dispose of stocks then held the Licensee shall immediately destroy or procure the destruction of the balance of the Licensed Product(s) then remaining in stock or in the process of manufacture and shall furnish to the Museum a certificate in a form acceptable to the Museum evidencing such destruction and signed by an officer of the Licensee or by an independent third party as the Museum may require.

15. **Rights to the Property**

15.1 The Licensee hereby covenants:

15.1.1 that it will not at any time after it ceases to be entitled to use the Property under the terms of this Licence use the Property in any manner whatsoever or claim or assist others to claim any right to prevent the use of the Property by others;

15.1.2 that in the event of the use by the Licensee of the Property in accordance with the terms of this Licence giving rise to any right to use trade mark names, trade names, copyright or any similar rights or privileges in the Licensee to the use of the Property under any statute or under the common law it will forthwith upon ceasing to be entitled to use the Property under the terms of this Licence assign any and all such rights to the Museum without payment therefor by the Museum;

15.1.3 without restricting the generality of sub-clause 15.1.2 of this clause that it will cede, assign and transfer its right to use the Property or any registered trade mark to the Museum or any nominee of the Museum;

15.1.4 that should it fail or refuse to sign any documents in order to give effect to any cession and/or assignment and/or transfer referred to in sub-clauses 15.1.2 or 15.1.3 of this clause within three days after being requested by the Museum or its agents so to do then the Museum shall be entitled to sign the necessary cession assignment or transfer for and on behalf of the Licensee and to this end the Licensee hereby irrevocably appoints the Museum with power of substitution as its attorney to sign all such documents as may be required in order to give effect to this clause.

16. No Assignment

16.1 The Licensee may not assign or license the benefit of this Agreement without the prior consent in writing of the Museum.

16.2 The Licensee shall not without the prior written approval of the Museum make available to others any standard specifications of the Property and/or instructions received from the Museum which the Licensee hereby agrees shall be confidential.

17. Address for Payment

17.1 All monies payable hereunder shall be paid by the Licensee to the Museum or as the Museum shall from time to time otherwise direct in writing and all consents and approvals required by the Licensee and notices to be given to the Museum shall be requested of or given to the Museum as its address aforesaid unless the Museum shall otherwise so notify the Licensee.

18. Confidentiality

Each party undertakes to keep and treat as confidential and not disclose to any third party, any information relating to the business or trade secrets of the other, nor make use of such information for any purpose whatsoever, except to those employees of the party who need to know for the purposes of this Agreement, provided that the foregoing obligation shall not extend to information which is:

(a) in or comes into the public domain other than by breach of this Agreement;

(b) in the possession of the one party prior to receipt from the other party;

(c) received bona fide by one party from a third party not receiving the information directly or indirectly from the other party.

However nothing in this Agreement shall operate so as to prevent either party or any of its staff from making use of know-how acquired, principles learned or experience gained during the execution of the Agreement. This Clause is binding during the Licence Term and for a period of 3 (three) years after termination and each party shall so bind its directors and employees.

19. Notices

All notices required to be given hereunder shall be given in writing to the recipient at the address stated on the face of this Agreement, or to such other address as the recipient may from time to time specify in writing by sending the same by pre-paid postage or facsimile and shall if sent by post be deemed to be delivered 48 (forty eight) hours after posting and if sent by facsimile, shall be deemed to have been received at the time of delivery as indicated on the facsimile activity report.

20. Remedies and Waivers

20.1 No delay or omission on the part of either party in exercising any right, power or remedy provided by law or under this Agreement shall:

(a) impair such right, power or remedy; or

(b) operate as a waiver thereof.

20.2 The single or partial exercise of any right, power or remedy provided by law or under this Agreement shall not preclude any other further exercise thereof or the exercise of any other right, power or remedy.

20.3 The rights, powers and remedies provided in this Agreement are cumulative and not exclusive of any rights, powers and remedies provided by law.

21. Invalidity and Severability

If at any time any provision of this Agreement is or becomes illegal, invalid or unenforceable in any respect under the law of any jurisdiction, that shall not affect or impair:

21.1 the legality, validity or enforceability in that jurisdiction of any other provision of this Agreement; or

21.2 the legality, validity or enforceability under the law of any other jurisdiction of that or any other provision of this Agreement.

22. Entire Agreement

22.1 This Agreement constitutes the whole and only Agreement between the parties relating to the Property and, save to the extent repeated in this Agreement, supersedes and extinguishes any prior drafts, agreements, undertakings, representations, warranties and arrangements of any nature whatsoever, whether or not in writing, relating thereto.

22.2 Each party acknowledges that in entering into this Agreement on the terms set out in this Agreement, it is not relying upon any representation, warranty, promise or assurance made or given by any other party or any other person, whether or not in writing, at any time prior to the execution of this Agreement which is not expressly set out herein, and neither of the parties shall have any right of action against the other party arising out of or in connection with any such representation, warranty, promise or assurance (except in the case of fraud).

22.3 No alteration or addition to this Agreement shall be valid unless made in writing and signed by duly authorised representatives of both parties.

23. Law and Jurisdiction

This Agreement shall be governed by and construed in accordance with English law and the parties hereto irrevocably agree to submit to the exclusive jurisdiction of the English courts.

In Witness whereof the parties have executed this Agreement on the day and year first before written.

Signed by _____

for and on behalf of

in the presence of: _____

Signed by_____

for and on behalf of

in the presence of: _____

SCHEDULE A

Description of the Property

SCHEDULE B

The Licensed Product(s)

SCHEDULE C

The Territory

SCHEDULE D

Date of expiry of Licence:

SCHEDULE E

Part I – Initial Payment

Part II – Licence Fee

Part III – Guaranteed Payment

SCHEDULE F

Dates by which manufacture and distribution shall have commenced in respect of each and every Product(s).

Date Manufactured By: _____

Date Distributed By: _____

Signed by _____

for and on behalf of the Museum

in the presence of _____

Signed by _____

for and on behalf of the Museum

in the presence of _____

INTERNATIONAL CLASSIFICATION OF TRADE MARK GOODS AND SERVICES

Trade marks are registered only in respect of the goods and/or services in relation to which they are used (or, in some countries, intended to be used). An international system of classification has been devised to assist the process of searching. Classification does not directly affect the validity or scope of protection of a mark.

1 Chemicals, food preservatives, industrial adhesives

2 Paints, varnishes, lacquers, anti-rust treatments

3 Cleaning preparations, soaps, perfumes, cosmetics

4 Oils, fuels, candles

5 Pharmaceutical goods, baby food, disinfectants, insecticides

6 Metal materials, pipes, safes

7 Machines, motors, agricultural implements

8 Hand tools, cutlery, razors

9 Records, tapes, cassettes, videos, computer software

10 Surgical, medical and dental apparatus

11 Refrigerators, cookers, dryers, air conditioners, lamps

12 Vehicles

13 Firearms

14 Jewellery, precious stones

15 Musical instruments

16 Printed matter, books, paper goods, typewriters, artists' materials

17 Rubber, plastics, non-metal pipes

18 Leather, imitation leather, travel goods, umbrellas, saddlery

19 Building materials

20 Furniture, mirrors, picture frames

21 Household and kitchen utensils, glassware, porcelain

22 Tents, tarpaulins, sails, sacks

23 Yarns and threads

24 Textiles, bed and table covers

25 Clothing, footwear, headgear

26 Buttons, pins, needles, ribbons

27 Carpets, floor coverings, non-textile wall hangings

28 Games, toys, gymnastic and sporting goods

29   Meat, fish, poultry, preserved/dried/cooked fruit & vegetables, milk products

30   Coffee, tea, sugar, rice, flour, bread, cereals, sauces

31   Fresh fruit and vegetables, grains, plants, flowers, pet food

32   Beer, mineral water, fruit juice, non-alcoholic drinks

33   Alcoholic beverages (except beers)

34   Tobacco, smokers' articles, matches

35   Advertising and business

36   Insurance and financial

37   Construction and repair

38   Communication

39   Transportation and storage

40   Material treatment

41   Education and entertainment

42   Miscellaneous

4.4   THE LAW OF COPYRIGHT IN SCOTLAND

A.   Introduction

As stated in Appendix 4.1 above, the law of copyright is in principle no different in Scotland than in any other part of the United Kingdom. However, there are certain differences in some areas such as the legal terminology used in Scotland, in relation to the remedies available in Scotland for infringement of copyright, and also in relation to certain formalities to be complied with when entering into contracts governing the licensing and/or transfer of interests in copyright.

If Scots Law applies, reference should therefore be made in using this guide to the content of this section. In addition, when preparing agreements based on the styles in Appendix 4 and/or when considering taking action for infringement of copyright, consideration should be given to the points outlined in this Appendix.

We would recommend that, in addition to making reference to the contents of this Appendix, the advice of a Scots lawyer should be sought in relation to enforcing specific rights in copyright works through the Scottish courts, and prior to entering into any agreement which is subject to Scots Law.

B.   General

This guide has been written from an English Law perspective. Whilst the statutes referred to in this guide are generally applicable in both Scotland and England, there are certain differences which must be borne in mind when reading this guide, as follows:

(a)   Copyright, Designs and Patents Act 1988 (the '1998 Act')

The 1988 Act is, in the main, applicable in both England and Scotland. However, sections 287 to 292 inclusive extend to England and Wales only. These sections however relate to the powers and proceedings of the patents county courts in England and Wales and are not therefore of relevance to those reading this guide.

(b)   National Heritage Act 1983 (the '1983 Act')

The 1983 Act does not extend to Scotland, except in so far as it amends or repeals any previous act which extends to Scotland and also except in so far as section 37 of the 1983 Act gives power to amend any previous acts which extend to Scotland.

(c)   Museums and Galleries Act 1992 (the '1992 Act')

It should be noted that only sections 6, 7, 8, 10 and 11 of the 1992 Act, together with Schedules 5 and 6 and parts of Schedules 8 and 9 to the 1992 Act, extend to Scotland.

The limited extent of both the 1983 and 1992 Acts under Scots Law should be noted when reading the introductory section to the guide.

C.   Remedies

In principle, the remedies outlined in this guide for unauthorised use of copyright works are available also in Scotland. The remedies in Scotland are similar but not necessarily obtained through the same procedures.

In addition, in relation to the availability of remedies and, in particular, the courts' attitude to the granting of remedies, the courts in England have recently given guidance as to the circumstances which they might examine when considering the remedies available to a plaintiff in a copyright infringement action (see the case of Microsoft Corporation v Plato Technology Limited).

In that case the court took what they considered to be a realistic view of the conduct of Plato Technology Limited in considering the extent of the relief it granted to Microsoft Corporation. The case demonstrated that an unwitting infringer who acts reasonably, notwithstanding that they were guilty of infringing copyright, can expect leniency from the courts in England.

It is not clear, however, whether similar principles to those discussed in the Microsoft case would be applied by the Scottish courts. The English court referred to principles of 'equity' in the Microsoft judgement, a concept which is not recognised under Scots Law, and it may be therefore that the courts in Scotland do not take a similar view on the point in question. On a separate but related note however generally speaking an interim interdict can be obtained faster in Scotland than in England and Wales.

Looking at the question of remedies as a whole therefore, separate legal advice should always be taken in relation to each set of circumstances where a remedy is required from the Scottish courts in the event of copyright infringement.

D. Terminology

The principal differences in terminology between Scots Law and English Law are outlined in the 1988 Act. These are outlined below:

English Law Term	Scots Law Term
Account of profits	Accounting and payment of profits
Accounts	Count, reckoning and payment
Assignment	Assignation
Costs	Expenses
Defendant	Defender
Delivery up	Delivery
Estoppel	Personal bar
Injunction	Interdict
Interlocutory	Interim remedy
Plaintiff	Pursuer

The alternative terminology provided above in relation to Scots Law should be read in tandem with the part of the guide referring to remedies for infringement of copyright. The alternative terminology and comments relating to remedies above, should not however be taken as a substitute for obtaining specific legal advice in relation to the appropriate court remedies which could be used in the event of a particular infringement of copyright.

E. Style agreements

There are a number of style agreements in the guide which have been prepared for use in England and Wales. The styles could also be suitable for use in Scotland subject to the following general comments:

(i)   all references to assignment should be read as references to 'assignation';

(ii) where the style agreements provide for payment of interest on late payments, the interest rate referred to should more correctly refer to a certain percentage above the base rate of a Scottish clearing bank, for example The Royal Bank of Scotland plc;

(iii) the governing law clause of the agreements should read Scotland as opposed to England and Wales. This will mean that the rules and principles applied by the Courts when interpreting the contract will be those of Scots Law. It will not necessarily mean that, in the event of any dispute relating to the contract in question, the dispute requires to be argued in a Scottish court. To provide for this the following wording should be inserted:

'and the parties hereto hereby submit to the exclusive jurisdiction of the Scottish Courts.'

143

(iv) in addition, whilst, in the main, the style agreements do not provide specifically for exclusion of liability for death or personal injury which may somehow arise through operation of the agreements, it should be noted that, under the Unfair Contract Terms Act 1977 ('UCTA') it is not permitted under Scots Law to exclude liability for death or personal injury. In addition, the rules relating to exclusion of liability for other loss under UCTA differ between Scotland and England. If agreements which are being entered into have provisions relating to exclusion of liability, and the provisions of UCTA apply, the specific provisions of UCTA in relation to Scots Law agreements, rather than English Law agreements, should be adhered to; and

(v) as a further general comment, alternative provisions relating to termination, and specifically the provisions permitting termination in the event of the insolvency/bankruptcy, etc. of either party may require to be inserted where the agreement is to be subject to Scots Law. For example, personal bankruptcy in Scotland is governed by the Bankruptcy (Scotland) Act 1985. Reference should therefore be made to this statute in relation to personal bankruptcy rather than a reference to the making of a bankruptcy order in terms of the Insolvency Act 1986.

There are also a number of more practical issues which require to be borne in mind when preparing and entering into agreements in Scotland, as referred to below.

F. Format and signing of agreements

1. *How do you constitute a contract in Scotland?*

The format of English contracts may differ from that of Scottish contracts. For example, there is no distinction under Scots Law between contracts and deeds and, subject to there being sufficient evidence of agreement on the main parts of a contract (i.e. price, subject matter and the obligations of the parties) a contract can be constituted by an exchange of letters.

An agreement can be in a number of formats. Subject to the comments at 6 below relating to witnessing of agreements, agreements transferring or licensing copyright do not require to be witnessed. Witnessing does not affect the contractual status of a document. What it does do however is make the document self proving (see below for a more detailed explanation of this). It is certainly best practice, where possible, to get agreements signed.

In addition, it should be noted, as under English Law, there are no special requirements for assigning copyright in a work. Indeed, if the agreement in question is simply conferring rights on the assignee, the assignee does not in fact require to sign the document.

Therefore, the comments in the main part of the guide in relation to duration and enforceability of exclusive licences (see page 6 of section 2.4) do not apply to non-exclusive licences entered into under Scots Law. Provided the licence has been put in writing and is signed by or on behalf of the licenser, the obligations contained in the licence will have full legal effect without the need for any further legal formalities to be adhered to.

144

2.   *How is a contract constituted in a letter format?*

Whilst it is often simpler and preferable to use a more formal agreement, if the licence agreement or other agreement is prepared in a letter format on the headed notepaper of either one of the parties, then the letter should be signed for and on behalf of that party, and a docket attached to the bottom of the letter. The docket should have a space for the signature of an authorised signatory of the other party to be added, together with a space for the date of signing. The letter should be prepared in duplicate and both copies should be signed by both parties. Each party should thereafter keep one copy each of the countersigned letter.

Agreements can also be constituted by an exchange of letters, one confirming acceptance of terms set out in the other.

3.   *How should a more formal agreement be prepared?*

If the agreement is prepared in a more formal agreement style (e.g. see the style used for the 'Book Publishing Agreement'), and is to be subject to Scots Law, the date of the agreement will (if not otherwise stated) be the last date on which the parties sign the agreement. A separate commencement date can be specified in the agreement, which commencement date can be prior to the date of the last signature of the agreement. A space for the date at the top of the front page of the agreement is not therefore appropriate for Scots Law agreements.

4.   *Identification of the parties*

The parties to any agreement should be fully identified, including the legal status of both parties (i.e. individual, partnership, company, etc.) and all relevant details including address of registered office and company number (if a company) and home address, etc. if an individual. Scots Law requires that both parties sign on the last page of the agreement itself (excluding any schedules). The signature of one of the parties (but not necessarily both or all) must be on a page on which there is text of the agreement. Therefore, a page break should be inserted (if required) prior to the last clause of the agreement to ensure that the text of the agreement runs onto the signing page.

5.   *How should agreements be signed?*

Requirements relating to execution of agreements by companies are the same in Scotland as in England. Under Scots Law, if one of the parties to an agreement is a partnership, ideally the individual signatures of the partners in addition to a signature for and on behalf of the partnership should be obtained.

6.   *Should agreements be witnessed?*

Under Scots Law, whilst a document is valid as soon as it is subscribed by the parties or, in the case of assignations where there are no obligations on the assignee, by the assignor, a document will become self-evidencing or 'probative' if it has been witnessed. If a document is witnessed, it will be presumed to have been subscribed by the grantor, on the date specified, and at the place specified in the document. Therefore, these facts do not need to be proved in court. It should be noted however that witnessing gives no presumption that the agreement itself is legally effective. The presumptions are concerned solely with the validity of execution of the document.

7. In Scots Law, the provisions relating to witnessing of documents are designed to protect against fraud. It is for a person challenging a document to prove that the grantor did not sign.

8. A style of signing provision for an agreement governed by Scots Law which is probative/self-evidencing is as provided below:

Subscribed for and on behalf of

[insert name of appropriate body]

by ....

a Director/Authorised Signatory

    Director/Authorised Signatory

at .... on the .... day of

.... 2000 in the

presence of the following witness:

.... Witness

.... Full Name

.... Address

....

....

It should be borne in mind that if a body is constituted by Royal Charter, or a particular statute, there may be more specific rules relating to how they sign their documents. This should also be borne in mind when dealing with companies who may have particular signing arrangements.

9. If there are any schedules to an agreement, these do not require to be signed if the schedules themselves do not refer to land or property such as buildings, etc., provided the schedules have been referred to in the agreement and a docket as suggested below has been added to the schedule. A docket can be added after the agreement has been signed, but must be added prior to the agreement being relied upon in court. Best practice would of course be to add the docket prior to signing. Suitable wording is as follows:

'This is the Schedule referred to in the foregoing agreement between Party A and Party B'.

4.5 PROSPECTIVE CHANGES IN THE LAW

The Proposed European Directive

Background

Significant changes to copyright law in the UK and indeed throughout the European Union will follow implementation of the European Commission's proposed 'Directive on the harmonisation of certain aspects of copyright and related rights in the Information Society'.

Currently, as this *Guide* makes clear, there are no provisions under UK law that allow museums and galleries to make non-commercial (or, indeed, commercial) use of copyright works, for example for educational, research, conservation or cataloguing purposes. Libraries and archives, on the other hand, are permitted to make individual copies of works for researchers (see the section headed 'Permitted Acts' in section 2.5 of this *Guide*). In Germany, museums currently benefit from an exception permitting the reproduction and dissemination of works of fine art in exhibition catalogues (§ 58 UrhG 65).

Overall objectives of the proposed Directive

The Directive aims to achieve a number of objectives:

- harmonisation of the right of reproduction, the basic right at the heart of copyright;
- adapting copyright to the demands of the Internet; this will be achieved by implementing the 1996 WIPO Treaties (the WIPO Copyright Treaty and WIPO Performances and Phonograms Treaty), which provide for protection of digital 'on-demand' transmissions by means of a new right of communication to the public;
- harmonisation of the right of distribution of copies of works so as to make it consistent with European rules on free movement and the single market;
- harmonisation of the exceptions to copyright protection;
- protection of the integrity of technical identification and protection schemes, based on electronic tagging of files, encryption etc.

The area of most concern to museums and galleries is harmonisation of the exceptions to copyright protection. One of the provisions of the proposed Directive in particular, Article 5(2)(c), offers scope for the interests of museums and galleries to be reflected in copyright law.

Article 5(2)(c)

Article 5(2)(c) of the original draft (published at the beginning of 1998) provided that the following acts should be permitted, without infringing copyright:

> ... specific acts of reproduction made by establishments accessible to the public which are not for direct or indirect economic or commercial advantage

The aim was clearly to allow libraries, archives, museums and galleries which are accessible to the public to make copies of works for non-profitmaking purposes, without having to obtain permission from the copyright holder or

147

pay a licence fee. This provision was limited to acts of reproduction, and could therefore *not* apply to any communication to the public, e.g. via the Internet.

UK museum bodies, led by the National Museum Directors' Conference (NMDC), were at the forefront of lobbying on behalf of museums and galleries. In Spring 1998, the NMDC commissioned a detailed submission which was sent to the European Commission, the Department of Trade and Industry, the Department of Culture, Media and Sport and selected MEPs. The NMDC submission was supported by the Museums and Galleries Commission, the Museums Association, the Committee of Area Museum Councils and the Association of Independent Museums.

The NMDC submission welcomed Article 5(2)(c) but suggested amendments that would clarify, and in some respects, widen its scope. In particular, it was suggested that the limitation should apply to acts of communication to the public, i.e. making works available on-line.

The proposed Directive underwent its first reading in the European Parliament in January 1998. The interests of rightholders in general prevailed over those of users and institutions such as libraries and museums. An *amended proposal*, revised to take account of the European Parliament's opinion after the first reading, was published in May 1999 [COM (1999) 250 final]. This retained Article 5(2)(c), but limited to apply only to:

> acts of reproduction made for archiving or conservation purposes . . .

The argument that the provision should permit limited on-line uses of copyright works by institutions such as museums and galleries encountered strong resistance both from the Commission and the Parliament. It was felt in some quarters that this would put museums and galleries in an unfairly advantageous position *vis-à-vis* commercial publishers, even though the NMDC submission had made clear that museums had no wish to prejudice copyright holders' legitimate interests or undermine the normal exploitation of their works.

Progress of the amended proposal

The amended proposal then went to the Council of Ministers which, as of 1 December 1999, had yet to issue its common position, in spite of the efforts of the Austrian, German and Finnish Presidencies. A number of aspects of the proposed Directive have been hotly debated – especially the harmonisation of the exceptions.

Once the common position is issued (perhaps during the Portuguese Presidency early in 2000) the Directive will go to the European Parliament for its second reading (expected mid-2000 at the earliest) after which the Council and Parliament must agree a common text. The earliest the Directive could be adopted is early in 2001 and therefore it will not be implemented into national laws until some time after that.

Museums and galleries therefore continue to have an opportunity to influence the debate. In particular, the NMDC and the Museums Copyright Group will continue to lobby for a meaningful limitation to the rights of copyright holders to allow museums and galleries to copy works for their non-profitmaking purposes, without having to obtain permission from the copyright holder or pay a licence fee. In this they will be seeking support from museums and galleries in the UK and elsewhere in Europe.

148

Index

commissioned works: copyright
ownership 30, 54, 56–7; databases 34;
merchandising 76; photographs 54,
69, 79, 107–8; standard terms 57;
United States 8
communication: reproduction 2
companies: contracts 44–5
computer programs *see* software
contracts: commercial publishing 48–9;
companies 44–5; legal entities 44–5,
145; licences *see* licensing; non-
exclusive licences 33; royalties 33, 38;
Scotland 144–5; unincorporated
associations 45
copyright: abuse *see* copyright
infringement; administration *see*
copyright management; art *see* artistic
works; authorised use 38–42; ©
symbol 9, 21; clearance 63, 64, 76;
commissions *see* commissioned works;
craftsmanship 2, 15, 72, 73; Crown
see Crown copyright; drama *see*
dramatic works; economic rights 3, 8,
58; engravings *see* engravings;
exploitation *see* exploitation; foreign
see foreign copyrights; history *see*
legal history; importance 2–3;
independent creation 11; literature *see*
literary works; music *see* musical
works; ownership *see* copyright
ownership; Parliamentary 27–8;
permitted acts *see* permitted acts;
photographs *see* photographs;
protection *see* copyright protection;
publication right *see* publication right;
quasi-copyright 72; reproduction *see*
reproduction; Scotland 90, 141–2;
term *see* copyright duration; transfer
of rights *see* assignment; University of
Cambridge 28; University of Oxford
28; *see also* intellectual property
copyright clearance: licences *see*
licensing; loans 63, 64; merchandising
63, 64, 76
copyright duration: after August 1989
22; anonymous works 23; artistic
works 22, 23, 24, 26, 31; between
1957 and August 1989 22–3;
broadcasting 22; commencement 20;
Crown copyright 23, 25; dramatic
works 22, 23, 26, 31, 73; engravings
23, 24, 73; etchings 24; European law
21, 25–6, 28, 31, 70; exclusive rights
21; expiry *see* expired copyright;
extended term 25–7, 31–2, 70;

fixation 20; joint authors 22; joint
ownership 25; legal history 21, 25;
literary works 22, 23, 26, 31, 73;
musical works 22, 23, 31, 73;
photographs 7, 23, 79, 89;
pseudonymous works 23; publication
right 21, 28; relevant factors 23;
sound recordings 22; transitional
provisions 21, 26; unknown
authorship 22; unpublished works 22,
24, 73
copyright infringement: account of
profits 38; authorising infringement
35; broadcasting 36; charging 36; civil
proceedings 38; copying 35; copyright
in infringing works 19; counterfeiting
37; criminal law 37, 38; damages 38;
electronic rights 35, 83; injunctions
38; issuing copies to the public 35;
lending 36, 63; museums and galleries
42; occupier's liability 37;
performance 36, 37; piracy 3, 37, 88;
plots 11; possession 37;
primary/secondary 37; renting 36, 63;
retailing 81; scanning 35, 83; seizure
38; software 35; substantial part 35
Copyright Licensing Agency Ltd (CLA)
39, 91
copyright management: access to
collections 52–5; acquisitions 60–3;
administrative burden 3, 5; assignment
57, 60; commercial issues 3–4, 5;
commercial publishing 4–5; donations
62; income generation 3–4, 5, 43;
lending/borrowing 63, 64;
merchandising 5, 53; picture libraries
78–81; purchases 62–3
copyright ownership: acquisitions 60–3;
assignment *see* assignment; authors *see*
authors; commissioned works 30, 54,
56–7; donations 62; employees 30–1,
45, 55–6, 61, 79; films 29, 31, 61;
first ownership 28–30, 32; foreign
copyrights 32, 44; joint authors
29–30; joint ownership 25, 30, 61;
legal ownership of work 10;
lending/borrowing 63–4; lingering
rights 64–75; not ownership of work
10; overlapping copyrights 65;
personal representatives 31–2, 34;
prospective ownership 31–3; purchases
62–3; revived/extended copyrights
31–2, 70; stockpiled rights 44; tracing
32, 61; transmission 32–3;
unpublished works 10, 61